UNITED STATES
OF
ANGER

WHY LINDA SARSOUR'S RAGE AND FAR LEFT VIOLENCE CANNOT MOVE MOUNTAINS

Hasan Ali Imam

Absolute Author
Publishing House

Publisher: Absolute Author Publishing House
Editor: Dr. Melissa Caudle
Associate Editor: Kathy Rabb Kittok

Library of Congress Cataloguing-in-Publication Data

America in Anger/Hasan Ali Imam

p. cm.

1. Political Science   2. Government 3. Policy

Paperback ISBN: 978-1-64953-090-5
eBook ISBN: 978-1-64953-091-2

DEDICATION

To my father, Mohammad Hasan Imam, who sadly passed away in November 2019. He inspired me to be just, moderate, and to have a love for humanity and its wonderful diversity. May God grant him Paradise.

"O Mankind! We created you from a single pair of a male and a female and made you into nations a tribes, that you may know each other and not despise each other. Verily the most honoured among you in front of God, is he who is righteous of you. God is All-Knowing, All-Aware." **(Quran 49:13)**

"Put Me in remembrance; Let us contend together; State your case, that you may be acquitted." **(Isaiah 43:26, NKJV)**

"Invite (all) to the way of thy Lord with wisdom and beautiful preaching; and argue with them in ways that are best and most gracious…" **(Quran 16:125)**

"Come now, and let us reason together, Says the LORD*…"* **(Isaiah 1:18, NKJV)**

"O ye who believe! stand out firmly for God as witnesses to fair dealing and let not the hatred of others to you make you swerve to wrong and depart from justice. Be just: that is next to piety: and fear God for God is well-acquainted with all that ye do." **(Quran 5:8)**

"Thus says the LORD of hosts: 'Execute true justice, Show mercy and compassion Everyone to his brother." **(Zechariah 7:8, NKJV)**

"And God invites to the Home of Peace..." **(Quran 10:25)**

"Glory to God in the highest, And on earth peace, goodwill toward men!" **(Luke: 2:14, NKJV)**

Acknowledgments

I would like to thank the following people who helped me over the last few months which made this book possible.

Robert John-Molloy Tasker (UK and Hong Kong), Lord Christopher (Nigeria, and Canada), Dr. Melissa Caudle (USA) and Kathy Rabb Kittok (USA), Helen (Italy), Chinthaka (Sri Lanka) and Zahbia Wasim (Pakistan).

Globalization at its best. Capitalism at its finest. Karl Marx was wrong.

TABLE OF CONTENTS

Introduction

Assalamu Alaikum Sister Linda,

I have come across your protests and listened to your speeches over the last few years with interest. I know you have a thick skin and can address criticisms. I condemn the abuse and threats you said you have received. You and I value freedom of speech, which is great about America and the UK where I reside; I am originally from Bangladesh. It is with this spirit that I write to you, hoping we can engage in a constructive debate where we may share the same religion of Islam (and trying to adhere to the Quran and Sunnah) but are resolutely divergent for our concept of human rights because of our divergent political leanings. You lean to the Socialist strand of the left, and I lean towards Conservatism's right. Not to be confused with the far right, who are not Conservatives.

I don't hold a political office, but I stood for Parliament in the UK in 2005 and have stood in county elections. During this time and during my time at the university in the 1990s, I interacted and engaged with people who had divergent views, e.g., Marxists, Feminists/pro-right to choose abortion advocates, Atheists, gays, Christian missionaries, priests, and rabbis. I am in the middle of writing a reply to the anti-pharmaceutical critics. I may also reply to the anti-vaccine lobby, who are purporting their views based on pseudoscience. I've also engaged with sects or groups from within our religion Shia, Ahmadiyya, Bohra, Quran-alone, liberal/secular Muslims, and even ex-Muslims. However, we have ALMOST ALWAYS ended in a good place, no matter how controversial the topics or the diversity.

Why am I saying this? Because dialogue and respectful debate can go a long way, it the ONLY way to resolve problems and achieve mutual understanding. My favorite liberal Muslim is Maajid Nawaz, a broadcaster on national radio in the UK, and a Hizb-ut-Tahrir member, a group filled with radicals. I remember when, during the 1990s, they used to cause problems in British universities. Maajid came out of radicalism and wrote that book *Radical* which is worth reading. We discuss different issues; we agree on many things and disagree on others because of his liberal leanings and conservative-leaning (politically and religiously). But we always respect each other's views. I hope that you and I can land in that same place of mutual understanding.

The only times I've had a falling out is with Muslim terrorist sympathizers and extremists who either banned me from their sites or refuse to debate with me and run away like chickens. A case in point was when I challenged the leader of Al Muhajiroun at the time in the UK when I stood for Parliament in 2005 as they accused me of unbelief for being a part of the 'kuffar' system. This sordid, despicable, and dysfunctional leader decided not to debate me in public and in front of the media, one week before the debate was due to take place.

A lukewarm dialogue took place on a local radio station in the UK a few years ago where I engaged with Muslim extremists in their attack of the UK Government's counter-terrorism strategy, which I have been involved in, which also was incorrectly misrepresented as spying etc. thus fanning the flames of mistrust amongst the Muslim community. The radio channel was a front for the notorious group I just mentioned, Hizb-ut-Tahrir (HT). Like Socialists and Marxists, they are good at organizing, harnessing many Muslims' emotions, and creating an extreme situation that leads to division. I wanted to confront this head-on, and I invited myself to attend the radio discussion. Afterward, when I asked Hizb-ut-Tahrir spokesman to engage in dialogue with some members of the Home Office (the UK version of Homeland Security), there was no response from her. However, her HT comrade issued a challenge to debate with the Government. He was playing to a converted crowd.

It is yet possible to debate and dialogue between divergent viewpoints without getting entrenched and showing mutual courtesy. The serious problem with American discourse is that people on opposite sides of political or social spectra have forgotten how to engage with each other positively and are often polarized because it cements them to their trenches. There was a breath of fresh air when I watched a conversation between Candace Owens (a Black Conservative activist) and Hawk Newsome of Black Lives Matter NYC. I also watched her lively engagement with the British left-wing/Liberal commentator, Russell Brand. That's how debates should occur. Take note, Liberals/Progressives and Conservatives in the US.

An injection of some British civility might go a long way to assure you we can engage in a lively and meaningful debate. And that fact that we are Muslims may offer some commonality. Above all, I am open to being proven wrong because that is how we learn. I am not afraid to change my views because I don't have an image to uphold with the masses.

Why am I writing to you? Two reasons. First, I was not meant to address this letter. I had touched on your views in a separate article that I am writing condemning the Democrats for some of their nefarious ways. I put that on hold now, given the current climate of protests, violence, and injustices gripping America and beyond. It made sense to separate this part of the article and morph it into a letter directly to you, given that you have been outspoken on many issues as a Muslim and Socialist leader, sharing your thoughts and rage about the current situation after the tragic death of George Floyd.

Second, given your outspoken views as a Muslim Socialist activist, I am sure you have a reach numbering into the millions. You have a large following, and since I vehemently disagree with most things you say, I am also trying to reach out to your fellow activists on the left to engage in debate. So, here we are.

Dialogue, debate, and understanding are the way forward instead of inciting violence, hatred, and revenge against innocent people who have solved none of the world's problems. I am not charging you with incitement to hatred and violence, but I call you out to support those who do. This letter should be the basis for an interesting dialogue if you have time to engage as I know you have millions of things to do; protests to organize, emotional speeches to make, people to rally round, crowds to rouse, and so forth.

I hope that if I ever get a reply from you, it will be different to the response from a left-wing feminist who threatened litigation because she didn't like the fact that a brown

Conservative male would rebut her point by point, but that's just my view on it. I have ordered and received your book, *We are Not Here to be Bystanders,* and look forward to reading it, *inshallah*. I have the book on my desk in front of me, and I continue to write this letter as your eyes from your front cover continue to stare at me with an elegant smile.

Weird, you are watching over me, but hey, I'm cool with it. I would have read your entire book before responding to you, but it was necessary to get the open letter out into the open quickly. I will also order the upcoming books by fellow Conservative commentators in the US, by Candace Owens and Dinesh D'Souza, and other forthcoming books by Dave Rubin, Ben Shapiro, etc. divergent ideas will be interesting. Don't worry, though, and I don't always embalm myself with Conservative literature.

However, I listen and respect some commentators from the left. I don't agree with most of what they say, but I have time for them. In the UK, they are Russell Brand, Nels Abbey, Yasmin Alibhai-Brown, Owen Jones, and Afua Hirsch. As far as American liberals/left commentators are concerned, I have enjoyed Michael Moore's book, '*Stupid White Men*' and his documentaries, '*Fahrenheit 911*', '*Sicko,*' '*Bowling for Columbine.*'. I also enjoyed reading Hillary Clinton's books, '*It Takes a Village*' and '*Living History.*' I did very much enjoy reading President George W. Bush's biography, '*Decision Points.*' He was an underestimated Republican President. I even visited a Marxist bookstore in London to attend a book launch. When I mentioned to one organizer, I was a Conservative and interested in learning other viewpoints, and she surreptitiously made a strategic withdrawal from our conversation.

I am mentioning this not because *'oh check me out; I am so well-read.'* I am not. And I still have a lot to learn from different people. I am name-dropping a few big names, so you know that I try to understand all shades of opinion and respect other viewpoints. You can assure that it will be pleasant and informative for us and those reading our exchanges if we engage in dialogue. Hopefully, this will encourage you to read on and benefit from this rather long letter unplanned. Please regard this letter as part of the courageous conversations. Hence this letter should not be seen as a polemic. I am seeking a serious dialogue.

With so many of you on either side of the political divide writing biographies recently, I guess I must start thinking of a title for my book on my world views and experiences if I become a celebrity one day. It would be *From Enrage to Engage – the Forgotten Journey Towards Peace.* Before I go further down appearing to trumpet my narcissism and megalomania, let us get back on course to address your views and statements, which do not appear to solve conflicts or injustices.

There are a few issues where you have stood by as a bystander, and I believe you have made irresponsible statements. I give the list of contradictions below. Although the George Floyd issue is foremost now in mainstream media and social media, I will still stick to the original format and deal with this topic at the end. As we delve into the arguments, please refer back to these two quotes below, frequently. You will see why.

"If you are neutral in situations of injustice, you have chosen the side of the oppressor."

(Archbishop Desmond Tutu, the South African human rights activist and anti-apartheid campaigner)

"What are the tyrannies you swallow daybreak that silence day by day and attempt to make your own, until you will sicken and die from them, still in silence?... The fact that we are here and that I speak these words is an attempt to break the silence and bridge some of those differences between us, for it is not difference which immobilizes us, but silence. And there are so many silences to be broken."

(Audre Lorde, feminist. You quote her words at the beginning of your book *We are Not Here to be Bystanders)*

Hasan Ali Imam

CHAPTER 1

LET THE DEBATE BEGIN

Contradiction 1*: Selective Condemnation of Sexual Harassment*

You are using your oratory skills to condemn Donald Trump, rightly so, but refuse to use your power of oration to condemn Joe Biden for alleged sexual harassment of Tara Reade... and remember that you burst into Brett Kavanaugh's hearing two years ago condemning him for alleged attempted rape and trying to defend women's rights? Where is your rage now?

In your recent Facebook video, you stated many times you did not want Amy Klabouchar to be his Vice President. *'**It's not going to happen,'** you said a few times resolutely. Why did you say this?

For readers who don't know, Klabouchar was one of the Democrat senators involved in the Kavanaugh/Ford hearings two years ago. Like her Democrat colleagues, they all believed Christine Ford, hence thinking that Kavanaugh was guilty. You condemn Klabouchar because, during her tenure as a Prosecutor, she did not prosecute any of the police officers involved in targeting Blacks. When you state that she can never be Biden's VP candidate, you are implicitly accepting that Biden will be the Democrat Presidential candidate. If you are so adamant in condemning Amy Klabouchar now and Brett Kavanaugh two years ago, why in God's name are you a silent bystander concerning Joe Biden? You should have also used the phrase, *'it's not going to happen'* for him. Biden must have a sigh of relief, now that his alleged sexual harassment is no longer in the media spotlight. A **'tail wagging the dog'** moment. And what does the collective silence on the left mean for the 'Me Too' movement? You and your colleagues are collectively urinating on this movement because of your silence.

Justice for women means support for all sexual harassment victims and not just for those whose alleged perpetrator agrees with your world view. You cannot be a bystander

CHAPTER 2

MORE DEBATE

Contradiction 2: ***Joe Biden's Stealth Racism***

You condemn racism against Blacks, and I stand with you. But Joe Biden's stealth racism has by-passed you completely. I know you are a supporter of Bernie Sanders, so calling out Joe Biden would have been an easy task for you when he told a Black radio host ***Charlamagne Tha God***, that *'you ain't Black'* if Black voters were struggling between Biden and Trump. I am not surprised by this view from Biden as this goes back to the old Democrats under Andrew Jackson, Stephen Douglas, Jim Crow, etc. which once supported slavery, the lynching of Blacks, the KKK, against women's empowerment, etc. When the Black vote changed from the Republicans to the Democrats after the Democrats implemented the New Deal in the 1930s, they took the Black vote for granted. I have seen the same psychology here in the UK where the left has always taken the Asian and Black votes for granted. The 'plantation' psychology remains amongst the Democrats in the US and Labor in the UK... that they 'own' Black/Asian votes.

Fast-forwarding to 2020, how dare White septuagenarian lecture Blacks on how to be Black. Democrats do not own Black votes. Period. And as expected, Biden then apologized but used a political technique known as 'pivoting' to deflect the racism by stating that he *'should not have been such a wise guy.'* What he should have said was that he should not have been such a racist. But that's left-wing politics, and before you divert to the right-wing politics, yes, we have problems too... but let's stick to your politics for now. Where is this rage or moral courage you keep on talking about? With your record, upgrade your anger to 'damn you' level concerning Biden's stealth racism and alleged sexual harassment. But an eerie silence exudes... and is deafening.

Universal justice means justice for ALL, even if it feels uncomfortable. You cannot be a bystander

CHAPTER 3

FANATICAL TERRORISM

Contradiction 3: Fanatical Muslim Terrorism

You condemn the White supremacists and also police officers who killed innocent Black people, and rightly so. I stand with you. But I do not see this manufactured rage and mass protests against some of our Muslim brothers who commit acts of terrorism against innocent civilians. Yes, you have condemned ISIS and Al-Qaeda but only online as far as I am aware and not to the same level of street rage and protests that you have engaged in recently. Islam and Shariya Law condemn acts of terrorism. I had my run-in with Muslim fanatics and terrorist sympathizers when I stood for the UK Parliament in 2005. As mentioned in my introduction, they can be challenged easily, and they run away like chickens.

I had a showdown of some sort when I attended a talk by a pro-Palestinian group at London University, and the panelists were the Palestinian activists, Dr. Ghada Karmi and the ex-terrorist hijacker, Leila Khaled, who was part of the Popular Front for the Liberation of Palestine and hijacked an airliner in the 1960s.

When I stated that the Twin Towers' attack was wrong and against Islam, there was smirking, skepticism, and howling from the audience, who heard and listened. One Socialist member said that a poor man's weapon is different from a rich man's weapon. He received a round of applause. There you have it, an anti-Capitalist rationalization. Hence, he justified terrorist activities. He challenged me back and asked me how I would feel if they killed my family. I answered him by stating that I would be furious. Before I could finish my sentence, there was another round of applause from the Socialist crowd who thought his views on revenge suicide bombing were vindicated. I continued during their applause, but they didn't hear the end of my sentence. I said that I would not target innocent people. It was a surreal meeting.

Afterward, when I talked to a few audience members and condemned suicide missions in Israel, a feisty Arab girl told me that Israel was a military state and that everyone, women and children included, were military targets. On another occasion, when I attended a rally in Central London held by the Palestine Solidarity Campaign, one idiot held an Israeli flag. Still, instead of the Star of David in the middle, it had the Nazi swastika. Right, that's going to help the Palestinians who are suffering. During this rally, I got talking to two rally supporters. When I mentioned the Islamic stance on protecting enemy civilians, she replied that I was not an Imam. Another guy in the rally said that he knew of an American girl who went to Palestine and saw the Israeli oppression of Palestinians and supported suicide bombing as a weapon. So, there you have it. This guy needed to justify suicide missions based on what this American girl said because he knows he cannot justify it according to Islamic standards. I am noticing that once Muslims get into political activism, they usually land on the left, which further disengages themselves from the Quranic and Prophetic orders to leave innocent civilians during wartime. Hence the Socialist/Marxist principle of '*by any means necessary*' becomes the order of the day. Sister Linda, will you have the moral couRAGE to protest and condemn Leila Ahmed and other groups who advocate suicide bombings, thus darkening the name of your Palestinian people? Or will you divert and pivot this scenario into the comfortable zone of freedom fighting?

***Universal justice means condemning injustice, even if it is against your people. You cannot be a bystander ***

CHAPTER 4

RACISM

Contradiction 4: Asian and Arab Racism

You rage against racism against Blacks, Hispanics, Muslims, etc. We agree. But then you tear the page when you have not condemned racism by Asian/Arab Muslims against Blacks and Whites in the strongest terms. **Correction**: you mentioned Arab discrimination against Blacks in your most recent Facebook video and also a post with the hashtag #ArabsforBlackLives, but not to the level of rage, anger, and protest. This is a massive contradiction because you condemned White liberal women for not protesting Blacks and only focusing on Trump's energies. You even said that their "hashtagging" approach was not enough, that they had to be out there and to protest. The same goes here. Your "hashtagging" of Arabs for Blacks is not enough. Follow your advice and organize and march on the streets with fire and fury against Arab/Asian racism against Blacks.

Just approach any Asian (Pakistani, Bangladeshi, etc.) Muslim parents tell them that their daughter wants to marry a Black Muslim guy... and watch their faces turn dark as if Judgement Day has arrived. Racism at its finest. I have not heard you condemn the Nation of Islam, where Black racists believe that the White race is inherently evil and Whites created a genetic accident thousands of years ago.

In 1997, when I was campaigning for Nirj Deva, the only sian Conservative MP at the time (now a Member of the European Parliament), we attended a Pakistani family party. During a discussion, one of the Pakistani guests stood up and said that he had a Black Muslim wife but had received hatred and condemnation from his fellow Pakistanis. It was painful to listen as he spoke, but I knew that he was telling the truth.

One further thought I would add while dealing with Nirj Deva is that he has been a victim of racism many times. One incident was from a Socialist politician. He told me that a top official of the UK Labour Party confided in him that one of the White Labor politicians was angry that this '*monkey who swung from trees in Sri Lanka*' would stand for Parliament in the UK. I was irate when he told me this, and this racism should be called out publicly. He told me not to mention a word because the Labor official who confided this in him would land into trouble. Nirj was too busy trying to win his seat to serve his constituents to be distracted by this left-wing racist. I know the identity of this racist, but I will respect the wishes of Nirj Deva and just let it go.

I mention this because the perception is out there that racism is the purview of the far right only. Yes, he shared his thoughts on benign discrimination from White

9

Conservatives and how he outsmarted them, entertaining to hear. I use the term 'benign' because White people are not racists in their nature but would use racist language, and they may not be aware of it. I don't know how to classify this, but I call it benign racism. So, they may use language such as the following (which I heard myself), '*he is articulate*' or "*the reason Africa has developed little technologically is that of the hot weather. Europe had to battle the harsh weather, which is why technologies had to be built to mitigate these, and that led to further developments*."

I was coming back to racism within the Asian community. In Dhaka, I witnessed anti-White racism during a wedding when our family friend married an English Muslim.

In 1995 at a university, I asked a visiting Black Muslim speaker whether he had experienced racism from the Asian Muslim community. It perplexed a few members of the audience with my question. But his answer vindicated my question because I know precisely how members of my Asian community think. He said that when he had approached an Asian family to ask for their daughter's hand in marriage, they refused and made some excuses, only to find out later they married the daughter off to someone else from their race and culture. His Black/Jamaican ethnicity was the problem.

I have seen how your fellow Arabs treat Asian laborers (Bangladeshis, Pakistanis) in the Middle East. Luckily, Muslim scholars have issued fatwas to ensure that laborers' rights are protected and not abused.

Another form of racism I have witnessed is not binary racism (i.e., targeting a specific race) but an attack on mixed-race people. I have heard many times that these mixed-race people have no identities; I listened to this, especially from

10

Asians, or that they are mongrels; I heard this from a White rights activist with whom I engaged with over a decade ago. THERE ARE NO NO-GO AREAS FOR RACISM. Anyone can be a victim of this cursed ideology.

You agree that the Quran condemns all forms of racism in the fiercest terms, but nicely (chap. 49 vs. 13). This verse, which I won't quote as I want other readers to do some homework and search, is the most potent verse against racism in favor of universal brotherhood. The verse is loaded with meaning and provides the best narrative of what race relations should look like.

Theresa May, the British ex-Prime Minister, quoted this verse from the Quran at the Conservative Party Conference in 2018. Unbeknown to her, the first time this verse was quoted in a Conservative Party Conference was in 2001 after the 9/11 attacks, by yours indeed, and is his favorite verse too. It is worth pondering this verse and asking ourselves whether we want a more unified approach when trying to resolve conflicts, respect our differences, and favor our commonalities or wish to be divisive along racial fault lines.

The far right loathe universal brotherhood because they want to preserve the White culture and don't believe in the genetic similarities between all people.... although ALL humans originated from Africa millions of years ago. WE ARE ALL AFRICANS. The far left/Socialists/Marxists divide communities by blaming White people and Capitalists for everything that has gone wrong in society. The same is for White supremacists who blame Blacks and Asians for various problems because of immigration.

I need not teach you to suck eggs regarding the Quranic verse. As I mentioned above, I am highlighting the inherent conflict that will arise because you adhered to this book and the Socialist/Marxist protest strategies based on racial fault lines, thus fanning the flames of hatred, which go against this book.

Oh, and that cream that is widely available in India, Pakistan, and Bangladesh? Fair & Lovely, don't get me started. I call it the racist cream. Why on earth do some Asians not like being dark and want to turn White? Yes, many Whites would like to get tans because it enhances their beauty. I joke with my White colleagues and friends who get tans that my tan is permanent and costs nothing... I have an advantage over them. But why would Asians who have dark skins have inferiority complexes and want to turn fairer?

Contrary to Whites who get tans for cosmetics, Asians with dark skins feel that they would be accepted more if they had lighter skin. Racism and inferiority complexes play a part is deep within our psyche. That racist cream should be banned. I know you, and I will agree on this paragraph, but the reason for writing this is that I am directing this to Asian readers who will read this open letter. The parents would do well to do away with skin color as a criterion when they look for prospective wives or husbands for their sons or daughters.

Coming back to Asian/Arab racism against Blacks. It is effortless for us to patronize Blacks by saying, *'my best friend is Black'* or *'we have protested against racial injustices against Blacks.'* You can, and you need to go a step further. When you find a wife for your son, and if he agrees, he should marry a Black Muslimah. There will howl negativity from many of your fellow Arab and my fellow Asian sickos... but this is real moral courage.

Justice is not just about preaching moral courage; it is about practicing it

CHAPTER 5

WOMEN RISE

Contradiction 5: ***Weaponization of Vaginas***

You rage against abuses against women, especially non-White women, and have condemned liberal White women for their latent and fluffy actions and implying that they are all like that notorious racist, Amy Cooper. But you refuse to rage and protest against honor killings and female genital mutilation that take place in some Asian communities (honor killings) and some North African Muslim communities (FGM)... which are against Islam. You did not at least apologize for stating in your Twitter feed in 2011 that you wanted the Bridgette Gabriel's and Ayaan Hirsi Ali's vaginas taken away because they didn't deserve to be women. When a young White student at Dartmouth College asked you about this, you used the same diversionary tactics and pivoting to focus on his White ethnicity which, was irrelevant to the question at hand, and concentrate on your track record on oppressed communities instead of what silly shit you said years ago. Even here, there is a contradiction. You question your tweet's authenticity and blame the right-wing media for manufacturing this tweet and then say that you said some silly shit years ago. Decide already. As you are so focused on ethnicity... your tweet as a Palestinian American was against a Somalian American ex-Muslim (A. H. Ali) and a Lebanese Christian American (B. Gabriel). All three of you share similar geographical regions. Aren't Lebanese and Somalian vaginas as privileged as a Palestinian vagina? The moral courage here would have been to admit you tweeted this and to apologize without reservation for the weaponization of FGM against your fellow sisters and be done with it.

***Universal justice means condemning injustice, even if it is against yourself. You cannot be a bystander of your own mistakes and a bystander of honor killings and FGM ***

CHAPTER 6

FANATICAL INJUSTICES

Contradiction 6: Injustices Against Non-Muslims and Ex-Muslims

Stop the Press: Sister Lauren Booth, who is the Sister-in-law of ex-Prime Minister Tony Blair, has been murdered because she dared to convert to Islam in 2010 after her experience in Iran. Her family was furious about her conversion, and so she was stabbed a decade later at her home when thugs broke in. One man who has been arrested said that the Boothe family paid him to execute this.

The above paragraph is fictional. I made it all up. But how did you feel as you read it? How do you think we, as a Muslim community, would have felt if the above was announced at a Muslim conference? We would have been in utter shock and horror and would have confirmed

Islamophobia. Now reverse this example. Why don't we get the same level of shock and horror when ex-Muslims exit Islam to embrace other religions or Atheism, who are then murdered, beaten, or threatened? Where is your rage in this? I have read ex-Muslims' stories such as Anwar Sheikh, Salman Rushdie, Ayaan Hirsi Ali, Ibn Warraq, Sundas Hoorain, Introverted Smiles (YouTube name. He is my favorite ex-Muslim), Ali Sina, Abdullah Sameer, Farhan Qureshi, Maryam Namazie, etc. etc. Sorry I am name dropping again. Some threats and abuses they had received after leaving Islam are abhorrent. Will you have the moral courage to rage about these injustices, which are very real, clear, and present?

While Muslims are suffering worldwide, we cannot ignore that non-Muslim communities have and are oppressed by fellow Muslim brothers. The Turkish genocide of over 1 million Armenians in the early 20th Century is a forgotten history. When will you have the moral courage and rage about these injustices under the Ottoman Sultanate? There had been widely reported stories of Christians in South Sudan being oppressed by the Muslim North Sudanese Government. Where was the rage from our Muslim brothers when a 12-year-old Christian boy, Iqbal Masih, was shot dead in Pakistan because he dared to travel the world to raise Child Labor issues? We have heard of Muslim terrorists blowing up churches or attacking Hindu temples (mandirs). But you will conveniently overlook these issues, won't you, because you don't want to ruffle the feathers?

You and I can agree on one thing. Diversity & Inclusion (D&I) programs in Western companies are welcome entrants to the discourse of mutual understanding. I want to see these programs spread to every company to gain a new awareness of others' life experiences. Such programs are in dire need within our Muslim communities where there some intolerance of non-Muslims, ex-Muslims, LGBT, tolerance of racism, and so on. Will you hold protests and call out our fellow Muslims on these issues?

Justice demands that you call out your community, even if it is uncomfortable. You cannot be a bystander

CHAPTER 7

PROTESTS

Contradiction 7: Your Attack on White Liberal Sisters

Following on from the previous chapter. More about fluffy White liberal women whom you were quick to condemn. You class yourself as a 'Progressive,' in contrast to 'Liberals.' Both groups are on the political left. Your gripe with White Liberal women was their fluffiness concerning protesting. You said in your Facebook video on the 26th of May, 2020, that you were trying to understand why they would only protest when it affected them and go out to protest against Trump. Still, very few of them would join the Progressives when protesting to support Black people. You are being divisive here and making this into a racial issue within the left. Here is Conservative telling you guys on the left to stand united and not divide yourselves along racial fault lines. How ironic. Although I will deal with your

18

reactions to George Floyd protests at the end, it is worth mentioning here that when I watched the demonstrations over the last two days. I saw many White women and men protesting in their droves with their Black compatriots to support George Floyd. There was a section of White activists who shielded Black protestors from the police. And I noticed a good few White women on the front line standing close to the Polices' guns, which were aimed towards them. Yet, in the last few posts, you did not acknowledge this. Bizarre. In your latent rage, you were quick to condemn White liberal women for not coming out when needed to support Blacks, but when they came out in force, this went off your radar.

Justice is this. If you are going to condemn what you expected to see, but you didn't, then you must applaud what you saw

CHAPTER 8

FEMINISM AND POLITICS

Contradiction 8: Feminism and Identity Politics

Your identification with modern-day feminism and gender identity politics is a significant contradiction and goes against the very book you and I adhere to. There is some convergence between Islam and some forms of feminism, e.g., the right to own property, due to be treated well, right to vote, directly to work where necessary, but here are also divergences. Islam probably aligns most with First Wave Feminism in the 19th Century, where there were demands for the right to vote and own property. However, like the old Democrats, this mode of feminism was within White women's purview only. Black women were excluded from this debate because in America, a Black woman, Sojourner Truth, had to travel throughout America in the 19th Century, baring her breasts to prove that she was a woman and had a right to be included in the women's movement.

Regarding Second Wave Feminism in the 60s-80s, there is some alignment between Islam (and other religions) and equal pay, respect at work but a complete misalignment for reproductive rights. Abortion is a no-go area in Islam (and all faiths... I did a cursory scan of this issue in Christianity, Judaism, Hinduism, Sikhism, and Buddhism, and almost all are aligned) unless under exceptional circumstances. In the Second Wave Feminism, the right to choose abortion is a must. Otherwise, one cannot be a feminist. You and your fellow Muslim politician comrade, Representative Ilhan Omar, share the same views on reproductive rights, especially the right to get an abortion or, if I say, kill a human being. And I remember watching your gate-crashing Brett Kavanaugh's hearing wanting to maintain 'reproductive' rights (wrong terminology... it should be 'abortion' rights because abortion is the opposite of reproduction). A massive contradiction, and this issue and Islamic/religious stance are mutually exclusive. It will be impossible to ride both horses at the same time.

There is further misalignment between religion and Third Wave Feminism (the 1990s, 2000s). The Third Wave has seen mutations mushroom into various divergent types of feminism. They are Liberal feminism, Radical feminism, Separatist and lesbian feminism, Cultural feminism, Socialist feminism, Eco-feminism, Black feminism, and Trans-feminism. On the back of this gender identity, politics has developed and mushroomed into various exotic permutations. The genders are Cis, Cishet, Trans, Genderqueer, Genderfluid, Non-binary, Orientation, Pansexual, Sapiosexual.

There are multiple lines of feminism being created, but the nature of one particular type of feminism can exhibit fluidity. The well-known veteran Australian feminist, Germaine Greer, wrote her explosive book, The **Female Eunuch**, in the 70s. It had an angry message. About 20 years later, in 1999, she came out with another book, '*The Whole Woman.*' What surprised me was that she had changed her tone in her latest book and seemed to mellow out a little. And there were more things I agreed with her latter book compared to her former book. What was very eye-opening was how feminists could turn on each other. In her book, Greer mentioned, '*The Whole Woman,*' about female genital mutilation (FGM). There was a condemnation of it, and she asked a very pertinent question.... why do we condemn FGM (which takes place in parts of Africa) but say nothing of similar self-torture that some women in the West go through when they get nipple piercings, vaginal piercings, and clitoral/vertical hood piercings? Good insight, and I agree with this observation. But during a radio discussion about her book, Germaine Greer had a short debate with a British feminist, Julie Burchill. It wasn't a debate. It was a catfight, and I should have got a packet of popcorns. Burchill accused Greer of supporting FGM. It was a bizarre accusation and twisted what Greer meant in her book. I never knew I would support Greer one day! So, even one type of feminists can be fluid and change their feminism in due course.

While I mentioned some alignment between Islam (and other religions) and some aspects of feminism and misalignment, there is a point of confluence between the four entities; Islam (and other religions), the left, the right, and feminists of the Andrea Dworkin kind. They can converge and cooperate like never. Pornography (Dworkin's book on this topic was perfect) is a point at which all the entities could have gathered and created a trajectory for women's objectification to end. In the UK, we've had our campaigners against pornography, such as the late Mary Whitehouse and the Labor MP, Clare Short, who tried to ban topless models in one of the British newspapers. They failed. Feminists and the political left and right and co-religionists had also failed. While the rights of women in the workplace and society are being recognized and injustices being corrected (as mentioned previously, D&I programs help people to understand injustices and life experiences of different people, whether women in the workplace, BAME communities, LGBT, etc.), in marvellous paradox pornography is getting harder in its candidness and women are forever being portrayed as sex objects in many exotic ways. This is an area where these four groups can work together one day, *inshallah* (God Willing).

Looking at the development of various gender identities and variant feminist off-shoots and fluidity in the feminist discourse, the Quranic narrative (and all other religions) of gender differentiation is straightforward. There are male and female. There are differences between the two, and there are similarities, but both are equal in the eyes of God. That's it. That is all the discourse that is needed concerning gender dynamics. Be proud of your gender/sex. But in the Socialist/Marxist (and its variant feminist off-shoots) narrative, there is no place for God. They see religion as a form of patriarchal/ bourgeois control over the oppressed working classes and women. The Socialist/Modern Feminist narrative seeks to draw values from their internal moral compass, spinning instead of drawing guidance from an external Creator.

Identity politics should be about being proud of who you are, the way God made you, and a basis for finding common ground instead of division and hate through identity politics

CHAPTER 9

HUMAN RIGHTS

Contradiction 9: *Abortion – Injustice Par Excellence*

You condemn racism and human rights abuses (abuses against Blacks, women, etc.) and crank up the rage-O-meter, and rightly so. In one of your Facebook posts, you condemned ISIS and Al-Qaeda for targeting maternity wards where mothers and babies were killed, and I applaud you for this. But, you advocate women's right to choose abortions, which is the vilest and evil form of torture than Mankind has ever invented (in fact, men invented abortion instruments) for innocent human beings. **No amount of oppression we see today and have seen in the past compares to the rancid methods of slicing, dismembering, or burning a**

human being. Islam and other religions condemn the killing of innocent lives.

In January 2019, in your home state of New York, Gov. Andrew Cuomo passed the '**Reproductive Health Act'** to extend the rights of abortion up to birth sometimes. The passing of this new bill was celebrated by lighting pink lights at the One World Trade Center. So, there you have it. A celebration of further injustices against unborn babies in a geographical location of Ground Zero where death should be commemorated and not celebrated; in a state that has banned the death penalty for convicted murderers. Work that one out.

Now here is a pertinent point concerning Black lives. There are proportionately more Black babies being killed through abortions than White babies in America. In 2019 the Black population accounted for 13.4% of the US population but accounted for 36% of abortions. In contrast, the White population accounts for 77% of the population, and 37% of abortions were White babies. I just touched on New York above, and in New York City, it aborts more Black babies than born. In Georgia, Blacks make up 32% of the population but 62% of the abortions in that state, whereas Whites make up 61% of the population and 25% of abortions.

Here is the point. The slogan **#BlackLivesMatter** is real, and everyone should agree with this and what it stands for. They should be allies. I would answer critics who say that ALL lives matter… yes, this is true, but it does not accommodate the unique experiences of injustices that distinct groups have faced. I deal with this slogan towards the end of my letter. But for now, everyone, regardless of political affiliation or ethnicity, should agree with that slogan and what it stands for. Now here is the part where there will be severe disagreement, and this is the genuine test of whether you and your comrades believe Black lives matter. This is where you need to step up and display your couRAGE and moral outRAGE that you keep on talking about. Do you have the moral courage to change the slogan to #ALLBlackLivesMatter? This accommodates all Black lives, including the unborn Black babies. If not, I would push back and challenge, WHY don't ALL Black lives matter?

You need to rage and stand in protest alongside the peaceful pro-Lifers who are often the forgotten defenders of the most innocent and vulnerable human beings God (Allah) has created? Ah, but then that's going to fly in the face of your feminist credentials, isn't it?

***Universal justice means justice for all, including unborn babies. Otherwise, your rage against other forms of injustices is rendered meaningless. You cannot be a bystander ***

CHAPTER 10

CONFLICTS OR WAR

Contradiction 10 - Israel/Palestine Conflict

You rage against Israel's treatment of the Palestinians, and most times, there is merit to what you say. But I have not come across your condemnation of HAMAS, which seeks to kill Israeli civilians through suicide bombing and drive the Jews to the sea. Your oratory skills are useless from the US's comfort when you should have the moral courage to go to Gaza and condemn HAMAS for what they are doing, using the Palestinians' misery to further their cause. If peace breaks out in Israel/Palestine, there is no need for HAMAS... it will be obliterated into oblivion (and arms manufacturers and arms dealers will be made redundant). There will be no wall either, which has herded the Gazans into a prison camp. HAMAS needs to use your brothers' suffering to justify its existence and refuse to hold elections since 2006 to cement its fake authority. When challenged about HAMAS's views, you said in one of your diversionary replies that HAMAS is small compared to the 2 million Gazans. Great. These 2 million Gazans have enough manpower to kick out HAMAS, right? If you were to protest against HAMAS in Gaza, they would kill you for collaborating. This is where real moral courage lies, not through oration from the comfort and security of America, but landing yourself in a volatile territory and risking your life to condemn the terrorist organization of HAMAS. And before you quickly and adroitly divert to the Israeli government's treatment of Palestinians, take note. Tens of thousands of Israelis have had the moral courage to condemn their Israeli Government on their territory and want to see peace with their Arab brothers. These Israeli peace protesters have more courage than you.

Many Israeli soldiers have refused to serve in the Palestinian territories. You need to do the same in your region... ah, but that would risk your life, wouldn't it? So, what is moral courage, then if not risking your life to condemn all forms of injustices? Recall that the late Prime Minister of Israel, Yitzhak Rabin, and the late President Anwar Sadat are the only leaders I know of in the Middle East who were assassinated by a Jewish terrorist and Muslim terrorists for progress peace. Sadat recognized Israel's state in exchange for peace, and Yitzhak Rabin gave up some Israeli territory back to Syria in exchange for peace. They have shown moral courage to the wrath of many of their countrymen and paid the ultimate price. Where is your moral courage?

You have also conveniently ignored the fact that Israel has Shariya courts to cater to Israeli Muslims (who amount to around 20% of the Israeli population) and is on par with the Jewish Laws (Halaka and Mitzvot) and secular courts. Israel is light years ahead of its European and American counterparts who condemn Shariya Law because they misunderstood it thanks to the Muslim terrorists and fanatics who have bastardized our religion. Give credit where it is due.

***Justice is about condemning injustices where you see them, even against your political leadership. You cannot be a bystander ***

CHAPTER 11

HARNESSING CONFLICT

Contradiction 11 – *Israel/Palestine Conflict… Again*

I like your mastery of oration, understanding crowd psychology, harnessing crowd emotions, and repackaging these tools into directed anger towards those you disagree with. I can learn a lot from you on this front, but I don't believe in protests. You were right to state in your video address on Facebook 27th May when dealing with the notorious White liberal, Amy Cooper, that "hashtagging" is not enough, that you have to go out there to protest. However, I say that protesting achieves nothing in most cases. Yes, peaceful and non-violent protests did work with Martin Luther King, Mahatma Gandhi, Nelson Mandela. You and I are nowhere near the level these distinguished men of the 20th Century. In your case, protests, where you justify violence, give you the feeling of achieving something when, in reality, nothing concrete has been achieved for the oppressed people you are protesting for.

Your power of oration and influence to condemn acts of violence will go some way. But you need to go further and use these skills to advance the cause of peace. Protesting against violence does not solve the violence unless you take steps towards achieving peace. Engaging with the adversaries in dialogue and mutual understanding (for those who want to engage) will help achieve peace and help oppressed people. This is even more true of the Israel/Palestine issue. You are from a Palestinian background, and you must engage in positive dialogue with Israelis and Zionists to migrate closer towards mutual peace to SAVE LIVES on both sides and free the Palestinians from this great wall of imprisonment by the Israeli Government... and also to free them from the clutches of their worthless HAMAS masters.

Do you have the moral courage to do this? Do you have the moral courage to achieve peace by risking your reputation in front of your people in the short term, by engaging in dialogue with your Israeli counterparts to accomplish the long-term result of peace and security for both peoples? Or should I say, ONE people? Jews and Arabs have one common forefather, Abraham... oh how all of you have forgotten this.

I attended a political TV show after the 9-11 attacks. The guest was the Palestinian activist, Dr. Ghada Karmi (I mentioned her above). I recall that she linked the 9-11 attacks to the injustices against the Palestinians. I commented that we should look to religion to find the answers given they are descendants of Abraham and with more commonalities than differences because Jews and

Muslims are the closest to religious laws and theological beliefs. Dr. Karmi replied that this was not a religious war. Well, I never said it was, hence an irrelevant answer. After the TV show, I wrote to Dr. Karmi to invite her to debate her apparent justification of the 9-11 attacks based on injustices against the Palestinians. She wrote a polite letter declining the offer.

The recent Israeli/Palestinian conflict has nothing to do with religion. It is power, politics, territory, and tyranny. But they will find the solutions in faith when Jews revert to the Torah, Tanach, Talmud, RAMABAM, Mitzvot (our Jewish cousins will know what I am talking about). When Christians revert to the New Testament and Muslims revert to the Quran and Sunnah. What is most sinister and surprising about this proposal is that Orthodox Jews are more likely to agree with this than Muslims. Work that one out. I think it's because Muslim political activism is funnelled into the left wing of politics where there is a detachment from religious values (because historically, Socialism/Marxism is based on religion is the opiate of the masses) then it is difficult to engage in religious solutions because brute politics and mutual revenge get in the way. I can summarise the arguments from both sides in the last 72 years as follows:

- **Palestinian**: 'We send you suicide bombers because you bombed us!'
- **Israeli**: 'Ah, but we bombed you because you sent us suicide bombers and rockets.'
- **Palestinian** 'But wait, we sent you suicide bombers because you bombed us and killed innocent people!'.
- **Israeli**: 'Well, we had to respond to HAMAS (or PLO previously) who are using innocent people because you sent suicide bombers and rockets.'
- **Palestinian** 'But you bombed us!'
- **Israeli:** 'But you did suicide missions.'

- **Palestinian** 'But you stole our land!'
- **Israeli:** 'No, it was our land originally.'
- **Palestinian** 'No, it's not!'
- **Israeli:** 'Yes, it is.'
- **Palestinian** 'No, it's not!'
- **Israeli**: 'Yes, it is.'
- **Palestinian** 'F*** you!'
- **Israeli:** 'F*** you back.'

Groundhog Day.

For the sake of future generations, the narrative needs to change urgently. Before you mention it, I am well aware of Miko Peled, an Israeli-American and son of an Israeli General. He is an outspoken supporter of Palestinians after reconsidering when he visited Gaza. I know where he is coming from, and I get it. But I will maintain that the Holy Land does not belong to the Palestinians and does not belong to the Israelis. You heard me right. Please ask me to clarify what I mean by this.

To close this topic, during the 9/11 attacks, Tony Robbins held a seminar. There was a reasonably angry Muslim who justified the 9/11 attacks. Robbins got him to talk with a Jewish participant. I have copied the link here:

https://www.youtube.com/watch?v=o9Hmr7-c5dk

In her narration, Chloe Madanes walks you through Robbins' psychological interventions to understand the Muslim and the Jewish participants. What happened at the end was very interesting, and I would like to know your thoughts on whether the ending was positive or whether it should have ended differently. I guess you would have chosen a different conclusion.

Justice is about recognizing the rights of Palestinians AND Israelis because Palestinian Lives Matter and Israeli Lives Matter

CHAPTER 12

GROOMING GANGS

***Contradiction 12**: **Asian Grooming Gangs in the UK**.*

This is a blight on our Asian community in the UK, specifically the Muslim community of Pakistani origin. The issue came to light only two years ago, although the incidents had been brewing over the last decade. These notorious gangs had targeted, groomed, and raped thousands of under-aged White girls. This is also a blight on local politicians and police who covered these up. As with FGM and honor killings, I have not seen you crank up your Rage-O-Meter protest against our Muslim brothers who committed these heinous crimes against these White girls. They targeted only White girls because of their racism and treated them as inferior and scum. I cannot work out why.

They should have thought of their daughters every time they saw those White girls, but they didn't. This issue was well-publicized and would have appeared on your radar. They have jailed all of these men, but I don't think justice has been done. Prison is not enough for these thugs, and you and I can at least agree that Shariya Law is more stringent when it comes to molestation and rape. Do you think it would have been appropriate for the parents and friends of these girls (who would number in the thousands) to express their rage and destroy Asian owned businesses with the justification that they will get insurance cheques? Well, you do support thuggery like this, which I will elaborate below when I deal with the issue of George Floyd and your ominous statements. Did you show your rage against these Muslim brothers? If not, why not? I put the same question to other human rights campaigners who were relatively silent here too.

***Lives of young, White girls matter too. You cannot be a bystander. ***

CHAPTER 13

FANATICAL BRUTALISATION

Contradiction 13: Torture of White farmers

White farmers in South Africa have been on the receiving end of brutalization and torture by some Black gangs who do not represent the New South Africa and do not define Nelson Mandela and the ANC's principles. This human rights issue has not surfaced in the mainstream media. During his tenure as President, Mandela tried to stop these horrid acts of violence, but violence increased after leaving. Forms of torture include rape, and I came across a case of an 11-year-old child boiled alive in a large bucket. Human thuggery has no shame. Will you get angry and protest against the torture of White farmers and their families? If your instant, lightning speed reaction is that it is revenge for Blacks' years of oppression by the White government, please let me introduce you to your racist self. If I am correct in my analysis, then this is racism buried inside you. Under no circumstances should they kill innocent White people for the crimes of the previous White government, in the same way why the Muslim community should not be targeted for the suicide bombing and terrorism, which some Muslim thugs have unleased in Europe and America. If I am wrong about my prediction on how you would react to the stories of brutality by some Black gangs against White farmers, then I take it back and apologize. In which case, I will ask you this. When will you display your couRAGE and protest against the abuse of White farming communities in South Africa?

***Innocent lives of White farmers and their families matter too. You cannot be a bystander. ***

CHAPTER 14

MURDER BY BLUE

Contradiction 14: *Other Murders by Police Officers*

Murder of Justine Damond by a Minneapolis Police Officer.

In 2017 the Muslim-American police officer, Mohammad Noor, murdered a White Australian woman, Justine Damond, in Minneapolis. He said it was an accident as he couldn't see in the dark. Unlike the George Floyd case, there were no witnesses here. So, we have to give Noor the benefit of the doubt. What was his punishment for second-degree manslaughter and third-degree murder? Just over 12 years in prison. This is not justice. You were right in one of your videos where you said that justice is the objective criteria rather than financial compensation. While you offered your condolences to Damond's family in the video, you lamented the fact that Justine's family received $20M in compensation.

In contrast, a Latino family only received $4M when their son was killed. Hence you brought in racial favoritism. Do you think Justine was a privileged White woman? She's not privileged. She's dead. If you were genuinely focused on justice, you would have said that 12.5 years for that police officer was outrageous, and you would have taken to the streets in a rage.

Suppose her family and friends went round breaking businesses premises, stealing and looting (as opposed to peaceful protests) of Muslim-owned shops to commemorate her murder. Would you have supported them because these business owners have recourse to insurance cheques? You have supported the looting by rogue elements with George Floyd, who have nothing to do with peaceful protesters. More on this in the last topic below. But I know the answer would be 'no.' But I see no rage, no pumping the air with fists, no crying, no shouting, no harnessing of crowd psychology against this injustice. Yes, officer Noor is one of our own (i.e., Muslim) but justice demands, and even you stated in one of your videos that you should call out injustice wherever it is and whoever it is committed by. Massive failure in adhering to this wise principle.

Who has heard of Tony Timpa? Police officers brutally killed him in Dallas in 2016 under similar circumstances as George Floyd, where an officer applied pressure on his back. He uttered the words, '*you're going to kill me!*'. The officers laughed and joked around him even when he went limp and was not responding. Although the policemen were charged, the charges were later dropped, and they went back on duty—an absolute travesty of justice. In Floyd's case, I hope appropriate justice is meted out to the police officers. Where was your rage on this incident? Why didn't Tony Timpa's life matter?

***Justice demands you call out injustice wherever you see it regardless of race or religion, and even if it goes against your narrative. You cannot be a bystander. ***

CHAPTER 15

BLACK BEATINGS

Contradiction 15 – Who Remembers Rodney King and Reginald Denny?

I am old enough to remember the beating of the Black taxi driver, Rodney King, by police. Riots ensued in Los Angeles in protest. On one occasion, when a White delivery driver, Reginald Denny, accidentally drove in a volatile area, he was dragged out of his lorry and beaten, punched, kicked, hit with a brick to his head, and collided with a claw hammer. While the police were brutal towards Rodney King, with Reginald Denny, they displayed their ineptitude by non-intervention. They did not perform their duty to serve and protect Denny. Given your natural gravitation towards supporting revenge attacks, would you have supported blowback from Denny's family and friends as they went rampaging and looting Black-owned shops because you believe that we don't have a right to tell them how to express their anger?

The above should not show the general state of the police in the US. While police brutality is real, as evidenced by the recent beatings and murders and many police officers joining with the protestors and kneeling down... they too acknowledge there is a systemic problem. Still, we should not generalize and accuse all police officers of racism. I remember watching a Black protester video with a sign in his body, stating, 'free hugs.' He was hugging police officers (Black and White) to the horror of some other Black protestors. He then replied to that critic by stating that one should not assume that a police uniform makes the officers racist in the same way that no one should assume he was a criminal because of his Black skin color. The critic was silent because he could not respond.

You and I know how it feels when after a Muslim terrorist attack in the UK, Europe, Australia or the US, that Muslims are tarnished, and we have to struggle hard through the airwaves to condemn such attacks and provide assurance to the general non-Muslim public that these terrorists are in the minority. If you still maintain that all or most police officers are racist, you are opening the door for Islamophobes to accuse all Muslims of supporting suicide bombing. I am confident that the police's number of murders is despised by all other police officers to protect and serve. As we focus on murders by police, let us also focus on how many lives the police save. Is that ok or is this even a no-go area for you just in case you ruffle some feathers?

***Justice demands you call out injustice wherever you see it regardless of race or religion, and even if it goes against your narrative. You cannot be a bystander. ***

CHAPTER 16

RACISM

Contradiction 16 – Another Form of Racism.

We have observed various forms of racism; I have highlighted some of which in the media and others I have touched on above. You and I are aware of racism shown in the past and present against Native Americans, Aborigines, Latinos, refugees, etc. etc. We see discrimination against Muslims (Islamophobia), where Muslims are tarnished as potential terrorists and suicide bombers. There have been reports of anti-Chinese racism because of COVID-19 originating from China. There is another group that has faced discrimination in the US and Europe. Does that group come to mind? Please take a moment to ponder before you read on.

Racism against the Jewish community (anti-Semitism). Did this occur to you straight away? If it did not, then please let me introduce you to your unconscious bias. If it happened to you, then I retract this and apologize in advance. Where have you shown outrage and the usual pumping the air with fists and organizing rallies, marches, and emotional speeches to condemn anti-Jewish racism? Not only have we seen this in the USA and Europe, but we see this in many parts of the Muslim and Arab world where Jews are blamed for the world's ills. Why haven't you called out your Arab brothers for their anti-Semitism? If I read you correctly, you are likely to fire back and say that your criticism of Israeli policies is unfairly classifying you as an anti-Semite. If this is that case, then let me re-direct you back to the discussion at hand. I am not accusing you of being an anti-Jewish racist because of criticisms of Israeli policies. There are Jews and Israelis who criticize their Government for their heavy tactics against Palestinians. I am calling you out for not condemning anti-Semitism in the strongest terms at the same level of rage, anger, mass protests you have expressed against other injustices. Ah, but then you might divert again to talk about the racism against Falasha Jews by European Jews. Yes, I know, but let me pull you back yet again, and let's deal with your relative silence.

Yes, you raised some money to fix desecrated Jewish and Muslim cemeteries…. that's nice. Where is that righteous anger you keep on talking about? Whose feathers are you going to ruffle if you were to organize a march to protest against antisemitism? You repeated time and time that one should call out injustice wherever and whoever it is against. Now is the time. Anti-Jewish racism is real.

*** Jewish Lives Matter. You cannot be a bystander to anti-Semitism.***

CHAPTER 17

FANATICAL VIOLENCE

17. More Contradictions and Support of Violence – George Floyd Aftermath

Under this title, there is a useful subset of contradictions in your approaches and woeful comments that seek to divide people. Before I delve into this, there is one agreement we can have. If no one feels sorrow, pain, or anger after watching the video of Floyd's merciless killing by Derek Chauvin, they are not humans. The media have only shown a part of that video; I've watched the entire video, which is gruesome. The people around the police officers were urging them to let George breathe, and even George himself uttered the words, *'you're gonna kill me.'* When the paramedics lifted his limp body onto the stretcher, you could tell that his time was up. The cavalier attitude of the officer in question,

Derek Chauvin, was **BEYOND REPREHENSIBLE**. The death of Floyd and ensuing protests which highlight systemic racism should have affected everyone regardless of race. It affected me, and my blood pressure and stress levels have gone up in the last few days. I discussed this with my boss, and she too had been affected (she is White.... but that shouldn't matter, should it?).

I heard the interview with the CEO of a multinational company on CNBC. He committed to donating $10M over three years to combat racial prejudice in America. I was pleased to hear this announcement and also his commitment that White men should listen more. Another CEO who deals with diversity and inclusion said, '*if you're White, then pass the mic.*' Excellent advice. Let White and Asian communities listen now to Black folks if we haven't before. Many companies will have diversity & inclusion arms and courses on biases, etc. Every company, which has these programs, should roll out these courses now more than ever.

I came across a commentator who tried to character assassinate Floyd by copying a quote from Lt. Bob Kroll, the President of the Police Officers Federation of Minneapolis. He stated that Floyd was a violent criminal his gun at the stomach of a pregnant Black woman. That may be the case, and the threat towards the pregnant woman is reprehensible too, but this does not justify what I saw in the full video. The police officers did not arrest Floyd because of his past criminal behavior. They stopped him because he had a fake $20 note, and an employee of a Palestinian-owned shop called the police as per protocol when dealing with counterfeit currency. His past criminal behavior is irrelevant. After release from prison, he turned his life around and came to Minneapolis to start afresh. Rev. Al Sharpton delivered a powerful sermon and eulogy and Floyd's funeral on 9th June. He had an insight that George Floyd turned his life around and was on his way to becoming an athlete. Floyd was not a millionaire nor a polished brother. He was like a rejected stone from a builder and that God chose this rejected stone and made him into a cornerstone of a movement around the world. I agree with the reverend's message and sentiments, and that's how Floyd should be remembered (and in the interest of justice, I hope that the pregnant victim I mentioned above got justice). So, let's nip that in the bud. I am directing this at the people trying to pick holes in Floyd's character.

In the last few days, you made many statements in response to the protests we have seen gripping all of America. Before I address them, I have collated snippets of your comments from your recent videos and posts on Facebook and Twitter. It shows these below:

> *"Our community would be out in the streets in the thousands or millions. Why are we not expecting this to happen? I'm just trying to understand. Are people not supposed to defend their people? Are people not supposed to be enraged? This country put this rage in these people. They have no other choice but to be enraged. Because this is not happening directly to you, you do not get to tell them what their rage looks like. That's not how this works. You don't get to tell people how to express their outrage. There has to come a time when people resist, and they may not withstand the way you choose to, but you don't get to tell people how to resist.*

> *This law and order business is precisely what Martin Luther King warned us about... People are more committed to law and order instead of justice.*

You don't get to tell people how to express their rage... Why are we not expecting this to happen? When you are a person who is not directly impacted by this, you have no authority to tell anybody else how to resist. This is not your place to sit there and think of why I get people and tell people no no no. Don't do that; he's not your son. That was not your father. But you know what, if it were your father, if it were your son, he wouldn't be wagging your finger, you'd be out on the streets by any means necessary getting justice for your family, and that is what these people are doing. You don't have to condone violence; you don't have to condone buildings' burning to understand why people do that.

...People are going to make sacrifices. People are going to lose things. People will be worried about their businesses; nobody should have to lose their livelihood, people are losing their life, actual human life... Do you know what an insurance check will pay for people's businesses? One day you will open and recover your businesses. These families are not together getting their family members back."

***

Your support of anarchy is as radiant as the Sun. Let's unpick these statements one by one, and you will see how irresponsible you have been with no remorse when you have been proven wrong.

17.1. *Your comment.*

'I'm just trying to understand. Are people not supposed to defend their people? Are people not supposed to be enraged?'

Answer: Yes. I felt the rage and sorrow watching the entire video of injustice against George Floyd was off the charts. But I did not go out setting fire on businesses nor steal nor loot. NEITHER DID YOU AND YOU DID NOT ENCOURAGE YOUR FAMILY TO DO SO. No one wagged a finger against peaceful, angry protests.

17.2. *Your comment.*

'This country put this rage in these people they have no other choice but to be enraged.'

Answer: You justified the vandalism and looting because America looted other countries and that America was founded on looting. America did not put the rage on people, America gave you the First Amendment, the right to free speech, and most people are exercising this peacefully. You also stated in a rally that you would speak freely because 'this is America.' That is why you and your family are there and have not returned to the Palestinian/Israel, that is why I am in the UK and haven't returned to Bangladesh, and that is why many migrants want to establish their lives in Europe, America, Canada, and Australia because of relative freedom and justice despite problems in these countries. The vandals and looters did not smash shops and businesses because of America's looting around the world. They exploited the death of George Floyd to burn and steal to cast disparagement on the Black community. Simple as that.

17.3. Your comment.

'Because this is not happening directly to you, you do not get to tell them what their rage looks like. That's not how this works.'

Answer: Yes, this is how it works. This did not happen directly to hundreds and thousands of people, yet they march to support George Floyd.

Your logic is very similar to some feminist pro-right to Choose Abortion advocates I have engaged with. One of them told me I don't have a right to talk about abortion because I am a guy and have no pregnancy experience. People can state an opinion even if they have not experienced it directly. I need not experience rape or assault to condemn them. You seem to be perfectly happy for people to intervene and comment on issues they have no direct experience of, as long as they agree with your narrative.

Those who are criticizing are not condemning the peaceful protests, which most protests are. They are blaming the meaningless violence that is taking place by a few people. You are conflating the two. Some of these vandals are White, and there have been cases where Black protesters were urging the White vandals to stop the violence. Whoever these White vandals are, whether prodded by left Liberals from Antifa or White Supremacists, doesn't matter. They are criminals, and they are trying to damage the image of peaceful Black protesters by reinforcing the perception of racists amongst Whites and non-Whites that Blacks are violent. They are not, and you should not be supporting these criminals who are using Floyd's death to steal, loot, burn buildings and burn the image of the Black community.... giving the excuse that America looted other countries. You are aiding and abetting such violence with your incendiary comments when most commentators and leaders have condemned them. So, why do you complain that you are under surveillance?

17.4. Your comment.

This law and order business is precisely what Martin Luther King warned us about... "People more committed to law and order instead of justice."

Answer: You cannot use Martin Luther King (MLK) to support your support of violence. This is another example of the selective use of justice. Yes, MLK once said, "***But finally, a riot is the language of the unheard.***" I do not connect this to the professional looters we see today. Those who use MLK to support the violence have been selective in his quotes. His method was obvious. He said the following on different occasions:

"Let me say, as I've always said, and I will always continue to say that riots are socially destructive and self-defeating,"

"Darkness cannot drive out darkness; only light can do that. Hate cannot drive out hate; only love can do that."

"I have decided to stick with love. Hate is too great a burden to bear."

You and your fellow left Socialists and Marxists should FOLLOW the MLK method instead of quoting him out of context to feed your divisive and incendiary narrative. His message was that of the unity of all colors and hope. He was a man of God.

17.5. Your comment.

"But you know what, if it were your father, if it were your son, he wouldn't be wagging your finger, you'd be out on the streets by any means necessary getting justice for your family, and that is what these people are doing. You don't have to condone violence; you don't have to condone buildings' burning to understand why people do that."

Answer: Wrong. Not only do you not have to condone the violence, you have to condemn it, and the burning of buildings. Excellent play on words in the last sentence to re-direct the attention away from criminal activity. Why support the violence when Floyd's family NEVER gave you and your comrade's permission to destroy livelihoods on George's behalf (not you personally but those agitators whom you support)? People, including peaceful protestors, perfectly understand why the violence is happening. Some Black and White criminals (Antifa or White Supremacy? Doesn't matter) want to fan the flames of hatred and give the impression that the Black community is violent, thus triggering a downward spiral of violence. If you disagree, then listen to the words of the officials below:

Mayor Melvin Carter (30ᵗʰ May 2020, CNN): *"I think we've all made the distinction between those who are peacefully seeking to protest and there are other people who are agitators who are seeking to agitate and incite violence. The problem we are hearing from a lot of our friends who have been in the movement here in Minnesota for a very long time is that you have somebody who will go forward and break a window and start a fire or something... then go back and run behind the people who are trying to protest and use them essentially as human shields peacefully. (The curfew) is designed to separate those well-meaning community members who are heartbroken and feel legitimate anger and sadness... and ask them to stay home... so that we can separate the people in our community who are hurting, who need to express their first amendment rights peacefully, and who are the people in our community who are looking to break a window and start a fire or create destruction in our communities are. Just because being a part of a crowd that the people who would hope to destroy our communities to hide in, that yes would aid those who are attempting to destroy our communities, that's the purpose of the curfew."*

Marc Morial, former Mayor of New Orleans (30ᵗʰ May 2020 on CNN): *"Later on we will get information on who is behind the acts of violence. If it is White supremacists, if it is Russians, other foreign actors who've tried to exploit the pain and exploit legitimate protest, this is a new level in our country. They should be arrested and prosecuted as well. (Quoting from someone else) Most of the violence is being carried out by people whose* *mission and values were not aligned, and they were not there to protest the death of Mr. Floyd but really to create havoc."*

Jeh Johnson (former Secretary of Homeland Security) (30ᵗʰ May 2020, CNN): *"Protest is a form of speech. Protest is a form of language for those who feel that their voices are not being heard. It is legitimate for people who are frustrated and angry and want to be heard. Protest that turned to violence, however, only emboldens and strengthens the other side. It emboldens law and order, extremism and militancy… it gives those on the other side of the debate the upper hand and cedes the moral high ground as MLK says an eye for an eye leaves everybody blind. We need to remember whether it is Los Angeles or Minneapolis or whether it is Hong Kong, protests are a form of speech, but protests that turn to violence hurt innocent people and cede the moral high ground and overwhelm the underlying message and gives strength and comfort to those on the other side of the debate."*

An official in Cincinnati, who was in tears (don't know his name): *"There are people down here who are encouraging 14-year-old kids. These babies are 14 years old… man, and they're encouraging them to throw bottles at the cops, and these grown people are encouraging our babies to fight. This is not their fight. I don't care how mad or angry you are with what is happening with the police. But these 15-year-old kids have nothing to do with these men. And these cops, Black cops, White cops… they did not do anything…. What I'm suggesting to the people of Cincinnati. What type of* *success are you going to have by attacking these people who have nothing to do with it? You got people out there who are encouraging kids to attack cops...they're using these kids, these are former students of mine... I am imploring that before these pops, and this gets bad... they just threw a brick at the cops, it's wrong, I'm telling you it's wrong. I'm so scared of these kids. These are kids! As an elder in the African American community, if any African American is encouraging these kids to be out here, they are wrong. These cops in Cincinnati did nothing to George Lloyd. This is wrong."*

Sister Linda, are you convinced by the wisdom of these people? Or are you going to maintain that they don't have the right to wag their fingers on the criminal elements? If not, then maybe MLK's daughter, Bernice King, might jolt you in the right direction. In her words below:

Bernice King: *"We can't keep doing things like we've been doing it in this nation, we've got to deal with systemic racism and White supremacy once and for al.,"*

"But the only pathway I know to do this is through non-violent means. It is a proven method. The end goal is we want to change and want it now. But change never comes through violence. It is not a solution."

Look at your statements I captured and collated and then have a fresh look at Bernice's comments. Will you tell her not to wag her finger and that she has no right to condemn the violence or tell people how to express their anger? If you still cannot see how incendiary your words were, then listen to Terrence Floyd, George Floyd's brother:

Terrence Floyd: *"It's OK to be angry but channel your anger into doing something positive or making a change another way because we've been down this road already."*

"Sometimes I get angry; I want to bust some heads, too," Terrence Floyd said. *"I wanna... just go crazy. But I'm here. My brother wasn't about that. My brother was about peace. You'll hear a lot of people say he was a gentle giant."*

"Don't tear up your town. All of this is not necessary, because if his own family and blood are not doing it, then why are you?"

"If his own family and blood are trying to deal with it and be positive about it, and go another route to seek justice, then why are you out here tearing up your community? Because when you're finished and turn around and want to buy something, you have done tore it up. So, now you messed up your living arrangements. So just relax. Justice will be served."

What is your response to Floyd? I am sure you are aware of the statements and resounding condemnation of violence from these people I mentioned. You must have had a re-evaluation and change of heart, in which case you need to retract what you said and apologize, or do you still stand by what you said? Remember that thing called justice? Even if it is against yourself? In one of your posts, you mentioned that security services are monitoring you. Well, I am not surprised! You are not directly inciting violence, but you are supporting those who do. It is akin to religious fanatics who support terrorism by rationalizing their actions. You definitely would have been under surveillance if you were in the UK. As someone who has been involved with the UK Govt's PREVENT counter-terrorism strategy, I would have supported this.

While the above comments from wise elders should resound across the lands, you are not hearing them (metaphorically); instead, you showed a video from another activist, Tamika Mallory, on Facebook on June 4, 2020, where she supports the violence and looting because of the looting that America did around the world. While the wise words from the rest are resounding, you have been cornered, and instead of apologizing you, clutch at straws and draw on Tamika to support your minority yet inflammatory views. But when push comes to shove, you don't believe it, and you don't want to admit it to maintain a specific persona. I will clarify and elaborate on this further down in section **17.8: *Your Statements That Justify Anarchy.***

I haven't mentioned President Donald Trump because he hasn't provided leadership or direction that the country needs. So, I have to revert to the previous Presidents, Obama and G.W. Bush, who provided words of inspiration.

President Barack Obama (edited)

> *"So, in a lot of ways, what has happened over the last several weeks is challenging and structural problems here in the United States have been thrown into high relief. They are the outcomes, not just of the immediate moments in time. Still, they result from a long history of slavery, Jim Crow, redlining, and institutionalized racism that too*

often had been the plague, the original sin of our society. And in some ways, as tragic as these past few weeks have been, as difficult and scary and uncertain as they've been, they've also been an incredible opportunity for people to be awakened to some of these underlining trends, and they offer a chance for us to all work together to tackle them, to take them off, to change America and make it live up to its highest ideals.

And part of what's made me so hopeful is that so many young people have galvanized and activated and motivated and mobilized. Historically, so much of the progress that we've made in our society has been because of young people. Dr. King was a young man when he got involved. Cesar Chavez was a young man; Malcolm X was a young man. The leaders of the feminist movement were young people. The leaders of union movements were young people. The environmental movement leaders and the tendency to make sure that the LGBT community finally had a voice and was represented were young people. And so, when sometimes I feel despair, I just see what's happening with young people all across the country and the talent and the voice and the sophistication that they're displaying, and it makes me feel optimistic. It makes me feel as if this country's going to get better.

Now, I want to speak directly to the young men and women of color, who, as Playon just so eloquently described, have witnessed too much violence and too much death, and too often, some of that violence has come from folks who were supposed to be serving and protecting you. I want you to know that

60

you matter; I want you to know that your lives matter and that your dreams matter. When I go home and look at my daughters Sasha and Malia's faces, and I look at my nephews and nieces, I see the limitless potential that deserves to flourish and thrive. You should be able to learn and make mistakes and live a life of joy without having to worry about what's going to happen when you walk to the store or go for a jog or driving down the street or looking at some birds in a park. And so I hope that you also feel hopeful even as you may feel angry because you have the power to make things better, and you have helped make the entire country feel as if this is something that's got to change. You've communicated a sense of urgency as powerful and transformative as anything I've seen in recent years.

I want to acknowledge the folks in law enforcement who share reimagining policing goals because there are folks out there who took their oath to serve your communities to your countries have a tough job. I know you're just as outraged about the tragedies in recent weeks as are many of the protesters, so we're grateful for the vast majority of you who protect and serve. It has heartened me to see those in law enforcement who recognize, "Let me march along with these protestors. Let me stand side by side and recognize that I want to be part of the solution," and have shown restraint and volunteered and engaged and listened because you're a vital part of the conversation. Change is going to require everyone's participation."

President George W. Bush's Open Letter

"Laura and I are anguished by the brutal suffocation of George Floyd and disturbed by the injustice and fear that suffocate our country. Yet we have resisted the urge to speak out because this is not the time for us to lecture. It is time for us to listen. It is time for America to examine our tragic failures — and as we do, we will also see some of our redeeming strengths.

It remains a shocking failure that many African Americans, especially young African American men, are harassed and threatened in their own country. It is a strength when protesters, protected by responsible law enforcement, march for a better future. In a long series of similar tragedies, this tragedy raises a long-overdue question: How do we end systemic racism in our society? The only way to see ourselves in true light is to listen to the voices of so many who are hurting and grieving. Those who set out to silence those voices do not understand America's meaning — or how it becomes a better place.

America's greatest challenge has long been to unite people of very different backgrounds into a single nation of justice and opportunity. The doctrine and habits of racial superiority, which once nearly split our country, still threaten our Union. The answers to American problems are found by living up to American ideals — to the fundamental truth that all human beings are created equal and endowed by God with certain rights. We have often underestimated how radical that quest is, and how our cherished principles challenge systems of intended or assumed injustice. The heroes of America —

from Frederick Douglass to Harriet Tubman, to Abraham Lincoln, to Martin Luther King, Jr. — are heroes of unity. Their calling has never been for the fainthearted. They often revealed the nation's disturbing bigotry and exploitation — stains on our character sometimes difficult for the American majority to examine. We can only see the reality of America's need by seeing it through the eyes of the threatened, oppressed, and disenfranchised.

That is exactly where we now stand. Many doubt the justice of our country, and with good reason. Black people see the repeated violation of their rights without an urgent and adequate response from American institutions. We know that lasting justice will only come by peaceful means. Looting is not liberation, and destruction is not progress. But we also know that lasting peace in our communities requires truly equal justice. The rule of law ultimately depends on the fairness and legitimacy of the legal system. And achieving justice for all is the duty of all.

This will require a consistent, courageous, and creative effort. We serve our neighbors best when we try to understand their experience. We love our neighbors as ourselves when we treat them as equals in both protection and compassion. There is a better way of empathy, shared commitment, bold action, and peace rooted injustice. I am confident that together, Americans will choose the better way."

THIS IS HOW AMERICAN PRESIDENTS ARE MEANT TO RESPOND IN TIMES OF CRISIS. President Trump responded to Bush's letter by tweeting, '***My admin has done*** *more for the Black Community than any President since Abraham Lincoln. Passed Opportunity Zones with Senator Tim Scott, guaranteed to fund for HBCU's, School Choice, passed Criminal Justice Reform, lowest Black unemployment, poverty, and crime rates in history...'*

I don't know what to make of this from President Trump. I would need to look into these policies. I am not so entrenched that I cannot give credit to those whom I disagree with. If Trump benefited the black community through these policies, then I will give credit where it is due. I will make some time to look into these claims, and maybe we can discuss this further in our next dialogue if we have one. If it turns out after fact-checking that these claims are true, then how would you respond? I watched a Netflix documentary entitled, '13th' about the Black community post-slavery and it had reclassified how many Black folks as criminals to put them in jail. Incarceration rates of Black men had increased over the last few decades. If under Trump, the incarceration rates had fallen, how would you and your fellow comrades react? I think I know how. You would divert at the speed of light to highlight other silly things he has said or done.

But President Trump should have acted Presidential and provide a message of unity, justice and hope instead of posing in front of an Episcopal Church with a Bible.

17.6. I repeat a part of what you said in 17.5

"You'd be out on the streets by any means necessary, getting justice for your family."

Answer: Marxists and Socialists are well versed in Malcolm X, who coined that phrase, '*by any means necessary*.' It is interesting to see how they remember Malcolm X but overlook the person he became, Malik El-Shabbaz, after he embraced Orthodox Islam (as opposed to the Nation of Islam, which believes that the White race is evil). He reconsidered when he went to Mecca during Hajj and witnessed the brotherhood of Man and people from all backgrounds and colors all equal in the sight of God. I had to remind my fellow Communist debater at university about El-Shabbaz and how he indeed found the answer to racism and disavow his anti-White bias from his Malcolm X days. **'*By any means necessary*'** is something he disavowed when he became Malik el-Shabbaz. Do you need a reminder of this? You know this. This is a part of what El-Shabbaz said during Hajj:

> *"(But) in the Muslim World, when one accepts Islam and ceases to be White or Negro, Islam recognizes all men as Men because the people here in Arabia believe that God is One, they believe that all people are also One and that all our brothers and Sisters are One Human Family.*

> *I have never before witnessed such sincere hospitality and the practice of true brotherhood as I have seen it here in Arabia. All I have seen and experienced on this pilgrimage has forced me to "re-arrange" much of my thoughts pattern and toss aside some of my previous conclusions. This "adjustment to reality" wasn't too difficult for me to undergo, because, despite my firm conviction in whatever I believe, I have always tried to keep an open mind, which is absolutely necessary to reflect the flexibility that must go hand in hand with anyone with an intelligent quest for truth never comes to an end.*

> *"There are Muslims here of all colors and from every part of this earth. During the past days here*

in Mecca (Jeddah, Mina, and Mustaliph), while understanding the rituals of the Hajj, I have eaten from the same plate, drank from the same glass, and slept on the same bed or rug – with Kings, potentates and other forms of rulers... with fellow Muslims whose skin was the Whitest of White, whose eyes was the bluest of blue, and whose hair was the blondest of blond – I could look into their blue eyes and see that they regarded me as the same (brothers) because their faith in One God (Allah) had actually removed "White" from their mind, which automatically changed their attitude and their behavior (towards) people of other colors..."

Malcolm X was open to '**adjustment to reality,**' rose above racial fault line and identity politics (as we call it today) and embraced the brotherhood of Mankind. Are you open to adjustment to reality and follow Malik El Shabbaz instead of Malcolm X?

17.7. Recourse to Religion During Times of War and Oppression.

If I have failed to convince you to separate the violence from the peaceful protests, let us have recourse to something we both are supposed to adhere to -- the Quran and Sunnah (Prophetic Way). You know the history, but I must mention a few things to benefit your Socialist/Marxist supporters who are non-Muslim.

Pagans in Mecca tortured the Prophet Mohammad and his, which is why they had to leave and migrate to Medina. It also is when the Islamic calendar starts. When he and his 10,000 companions came back to take over Mecca, what did they do? Did they loot, burn, and pillage the city that they would have a right to do in your parallel universe? When the

Prophet asked the Meccans what they wanted from him, they answered, *'**mercy oh generous brother.**'* And so, they were freed, apart from four criminals who received capital punishment. You will know the rules of engagement during wartime. What did Prophet Mohammad command? He said,

> *"Do not kill children. Avoid touching people who devote themselves to worship in churches! Never murder women and the elderly. Do not set trees on fire or cut them down. Never destroy houses."*

Now compare the Prophet's words with yours. Do they match? Let us read his successor (caliph) words, Abu Bakr, when he advised his army before the expedition to Syria. He said,

> *"Stop, O people, that I may give you ten rules to keep by heart: do not commit treason, nor depart from the right path. You must not mutilate, neither kill a child or aged man or woman. Do not destroy a palm tree, burn it with fire, and not cut any fruitful tree. You must not slay any of the flock or herds or the camels, save for your subsistence. You are likely to pass by people who have devoted their lives to monastic services; leave them to which they had devoted their lives..."*

How do these commands from these two distinguished men of history compare to your words? It is ironic how much we have lost in terms of our principles for fighting enemies in warfare. It had to take an American General (don't know his name but watched him on CNN a decade ago) to remind people of the Islamic rules of justice during warfare. But Muslim fanatics ignore these and justify suicide bombing and terrorism. Listen to a British colonel's words, Tim Collins, who gave his troops an inspiring speech before they went into Iraq in 2003. His speech is hung in the Oval Office. American generals and soldiers could do well to learn from him. I have edited the speech:

"We go to liberate, not to conquer. We will not fly our flags in their country. We are entering Iraq to free a people, and the only flag which will be flown in that ancient land is their own. Show respect for them. Some are alive at this moment who will not be alive shortly.... But if you are ferocious in battle, remember to be magnanimous in victory. Iraq is steeped in history. It is the site of the Garden of Eden, of the Great Flood, and the birthplace of Abraham. Tread lightly there. You will see things that no man could pay to see- and you will have to go a long way to find a more decent, generous, and upright people than the Iraqis. Their hospitality will embarrass you even though they have nothing. Don't treat them as refugees, for they are in their own country. Their children will be poor. In years to come, they will know that you brought the light of liberation in their lives. If there are casualties of war, they did not plan to die this day when they woke up and got dressed in the morning. Allow them dignity in death.... (he talks about vanquishing the enemy soldiers, which I have deleted).

It is a big step to take another human life. It is not to be done lightly. I know of men who have taken life needlessly in other conflicts. I can assure you they live with the mark of Cain upon them. If someone surrenders to you, then remember they have that right in international law and ensure that they go home to their family one day. The ones who wish to fight, well, we aim to please... You will be shunned unless your conduct is of the highest - for your deeds will follow you down through history. We will bring shame on neither our uniform nor our nation...."

Why am I mentioning Col. Collins? Because when I heard his speech, it resonated with the Islamic principles of Just warfare. In contrast, Osama bin Laden had urged followers to kill American civilians. His son, Hamza bin Laden offered, "***advice for martyrdom-seekers in the West***," where he advised Muslims living in America, the West, and occupied Palestine to stay in their home countries and launch lone-wolf terror attacks rather than traveling to fight in the Syrian Civil War. He said, "***Inflicting punishment on Jews and crusaders where you are present is more vexing and severe for the enemy***," and encouraged his followers to "***look for Jewish targets everywhere***," and that if none could be found, attack American and NATO targets.

Now compare the statements above with the commands of the Prophet and Abu Bakr. Who, in principle, is closer to the Prophetic tradition? Muslim extremists have departed entirely from the principles of our religion and the practice during wartime. The words of Tim Collins are closer to the Islamic tradition (and also the Christian idea of a 'just war' doctrine). Of course, we can talk about the bombing of civilians in Iraq, etc. and I am aware of Ramsey Clarke (former US Attorney General) who documented evidence of war crimes by the Americans during Gulf War 1 in 1991, in his book, '***The Fire This Time – US War Crimes in the Gulf***.' I know this side of the argument.

In 2006, when I delivered a brief speech to the Conservative Party conference, I condemned the then Democrat Secretary of State, Madeleine Albright, for stating that she thought the deaths of 500,000 Iraqi children were a price worth paying for freedom. Although she apologized later for that statement, that fact that she even thought about it in the first place, given her experience, is mind-boggling. It's something that a Neocon would say. Albright outconned the Neocons. So, I am well aware of the evidence of injustices in Iraq by Western troops, and these go against the very principles that Col. Tim Collins advised his men and against Biblical principles of justice (in the Torah) and *'Peace on earth and goodwill to all men'* (Luke 2:14). When President Trump held the Bible's copy outside that Episcopal church, he would have done well to read a few pages from it and act upon its principles.

Now, coming back to your statements about supporting violence, do your words closely align with our Islamic principles on justice? I know the principles are embedded in you somewhere. Still, your strong allegiance to the *'Marxist/Socialist by any means necessary,'* *'religion is for controlling the working class,' and 'religion is patriarchy'* narrative is quashing the Islamic principles that are bursting to get out. If we are afraid of God alone, then they would burst out immediately. But you have people to please and relations to uphold. You don't want to rock the boat. I get that. That is why I am rocking your boat for you.

17.8: *Your Statements that Justify Anarchy*

> *"People are going to make sacrifices. People will lose things; people are worried about their businesses, nobody should have to lose their livelihood, people are losing their life, actual human life… Do you know what an insurance check will pay for people's businesses? One day you will be able to open and recover your businesses. These families are not together getting their family members back."*

Answer: This is one of the most preposterous, incendiary, and insidious statements you have made that justifies anarchy. Anarchy perpetrated by White Antifa liberals or White supremacists to coax Black protesters to fall in the trap of magnifying the misperception of Black violence. What is it about peaceful protests that you do not understand? The changes that are taking place to start correcting injustices would have happened without the violence. Why do you undermine the peaceful protesters and assume that their messages will not get through? By undermining them, you undermine their powerful messages, and you also stick two fingers up at the very eminent leaders of the 20th Century. They moved mountains through non-violent protests and actions, Martin Luther King Jr, Mahatma Gandhi, Nelson Mandela.

Do you understand this? If not, why not? Let's take your above claims one by one:

17.8.1.

You imply that people should make sacrifices of damaged businesses and looting because humans have lost more.... their lives. When people claim they don't realize how demeaning this is to the people who lost their lives. In this case of Floyd, his life does not matter in the eyes of the thugs. By justifying anarchy, destruction, and stealing, they think they are doing justice to Floyd's murder. Think about it. The principle of equivalence is being used here...that somehow the destruction that is taking place is equivalent to the life taken from George Floyd. WRONG. Anarchy and destruction of businesses whose owners had nothing to do with Floyd's death did not equate to Floyd's justice. How dare they cheapen the life of Floyd by thinking they are doing justice.

Justice will be done when the four police officers get stiff sentences, when Floyd's family is taken care of, when his daughter, Gianni, has a bright future. And I hope Floyd's family receives compensation amounting to double-digit millions of dollars (in the same way that Justine Damond's family received) so that they can rebuild their lives. Please don't be patronizing and say that financial compensation doesn't bring back a life. It has nothing to do with the person who passed away. It has to do with supporting the families he has left behind so that their future is secure. I am glad that Kayne West has donated $2 M to families of George Floyd, Breonna Taylor, and Ahmaud Arbery. Gianni's future education will be fully paid for. This is how you honor the life of someone who was brutally murdered.

And in the long run, we honor the life of Floyd by making structural changes to systemic racism and provide opportunities that would be expected for communities that have fallen behind.

17.8.2

When you say that business owners will receive insurance cheques, you give the green light for any looting and anarchy because businesses will survive and rebuild through insurance. Unfortunately, you had threats to your life during your tenure as an activist, and it is horrendous for your detractors to publish your family's home address. Now suppose someone broke in to steal and destroy your residence. Would you tell yourself and your family that it's ok because your house and car have insurance, so let them break-in? No, you would call the police immediately to protect you and your family. Yes, you would, please don't lie to yourself. Hence you wish on others that which you do not want for yourself and your families.

You have also missed an essential point. Some agitators were White men dressed up in disguise, armed with hammers who broke windows. These White men may be White supremacists or White liberals from Antifa or both. I don't care who they are… they are criminals and agitators. Period. The Black protestors who were nearby urged these men to STOP the vandalism. Does your *'you don't have a right to tell protestors how to express their anger'* narrative work here? It implies that you condemn the peaceful Black protestors who were pleading with these White criminals to stop destroying property. Were these peaceful protestors dishonoring George Floyd by telling the criminals to stop destroying buildings? Please help me understand this contradiction.

17.8.3

There are signs that you may have regretted what you said previously about the justification for looting and anarchy as a way of justice for Floyd's death. I ascertain this from your Facebook post on 29th May. You posted a message defending the Palestinian store owner of Cups Foods, whose employee called the police after Floyd presented a fake $20 bill. I copy your post below:

> *"There's been a lot of misinformation on the internet about the store owner and the details of the events that unfolded before George Floyd was murdered.*
>
> *I spoke to Mahmoud Abumayyeleh, the owner of Cups Food, and local patrons and community members.*
>
> *Here are some facts:*

1. The Store owner is a Palestinian American, and he was not present at the store and was not the one who called the police.

2. There is a state policy that requires stores to call the police in the case of counterfeit bills. This is routine, and the police come, ask patrons about the bill to trace its origination. The police confiscate the counterfeit bills. Should be no arrests, no violence. (I still don't support the calling of police.)

3. Because of this known policy, an employee of Cups Food was the one who called the police - never expecting this would be the result. The employee also recorded George Floyd's murder.

4. The same employee called the owner, Mahmoud, to tell him that the police are brutalizing George. He then instructed them to call the cops on the cops.

5. Nephew of the store owner who was also at the store was seen in a video yelling to let George go and was pushed away by one of the Asian cops.

6. Cups Food has footage that George was NOT resisting arrest.

7. Cups Food DOES NOT sell alcohol or pork.

8. Cups Food owner is in touch with George's family lawyer and has given a donation to the family to help cover some funeral costs.

We can argue that police should have never been called. It wasn't worth it, and that would be my position. But they were, and MURDER/DEATH should never have been the result, and that is the issue here.

I understand that we have a long way to go to build transformative relationships between Arab/Asian store owners and local Black communities. As a daughter of a Palestinian man who owned a store for 38 years in Crown Heights, this is personal. These communities deserve business owners who are contributors to communities, not just takers. Anti-Black racism in Arab American communities is REAL. We have to acknowledge it. We have to eradicate it. This is work I will commit myself to.

In this specific case, Mahmoud and his family are well respected. He hires local; he supports the local community. Here is a testimony from one of the local young folks who patron Cups Food.

https://www.facebook.com/deon.price.73/posts/28 49875025090394

Let's keep the anger for now focused on where it needs to: on the cops who killed George Floyd, the powerful people who are protecting them, and the systems that need to be dismantled. The same time we can begin the important work to eradicate anti-Black racism from within.

P.S. the purpose of this post is to clarify misinformation because Mahmoud and his family are receiving serious death threats and his home address was posted online.

Edit: I removed specific details about the person who called the police because it was honestly unnecessary. The point was already made that the store owner was not who made the call. I apologize to those who were hurt, and I ask for benefit of the doubt that I intended to make clarifications and quell misinformation—sending love to all in these challenging times. My intention is not to add to more stress."

Why did you make the claims above to support your fellow Palestinian brother's Cups Food business owner? Because he was getting death threats. You made an excellent and elegant defense above and an indirect plea to anarchists not to target him or his family or his business. May God reward you for this intervention. You did exactly what anyone with love for humanity would have done. Unfortunately, it came short of a direct condemnation of the threats. Why? Because it will contradict your debased narrative that we have no right to tell people how to express their anger. Your above intervention on Facebook is doing precisely that, condemning the anger/threats, but indirectly. And when I saw the broadcast of the area outside Cup Food on 4th June, it was still intact, and they pleased me that the anarchists did not target this business. I know you were satisfied too. Please show universal justice and put up a similar post to support other business owners who serve their communities. Can you see the worst-case scenario that could have unfolded because of your support of the manifestation of rage and anger into violence? Thank God that the Palestinian owner of the shop and his family were not killed. If they had been killed, then you would have been partly culpable. Please take ownership of your mistake. That is what good leaders do. Can you see the inherent conflicts between your identification with Islam and revolutionary Socialism/Marxism?

17.8.4

Following on from above, when you said in another video or post, the large company called 'Target' will survive the looting because they have billions of dollars. This is just a rehash of anti-Capitalist trash. Socialists and Marxists dislike large corporations; hence, anarchists will try to justify attacks on them. Somehow the anti-Capitalist narrative is being slipped into the fray to link it to oppression. They cannot understand that every single large corporation started as a small business. So, if you and your colleagues are supporting small businesses, well, you are doing so only up to a point. When those businesses grow and expand and become large and influential in a few decades, you will treat them as enemies. You do not want small businesses to succeed.

About fifteen years ago, when I attended a Parliament meeting, the panellists included the Labour MP, Jeremy Corbyn (who later became a Labour Party leader until this year), and a Socialist activist. There was mention of evil Western multinationals and exploitation of third world countries and that they should leave these countries. During Q&A, I asked them whether they would ask Eastern multinationals (e.g., Japan) to go back to their countries. I also pointed out that I was proud that a Bangladeshi pharmaceutical company, Beximco, was expanding to other countries and becoming a multinational... should it go back to Bangladesh and not expand? There were no answers from the panellists, and so my questions ended up becoming rhetorical questions.

For me, this was a useful insight into some Socialist left, thinking that only Western companies could succeed, expand internationally, and exert influence. It did not occur to them that companies from the Far East or even from a developing country like Bangladesh could also serve .up successful multinational businesses globally. This is inert racism as they think only White-owned companies could expand, but yellow or brown or Black-owned companies could not.

Businesses, whether large and small, serve local communities. When you justify anarchists to destroy businesses, especially during the COVID pandemic where millions of Americans have lost their jobs, you are aiding and abetting the destruction of livelihoods of people from all races and backgrounds, and supporting the destruction of businesses owned by Black, Asian, Latino and White entrepreneurs who had nothing to do with Floyd's murder. Yet you and your supporters dare to justify the destruction of livelihoods because this is meant to be equivalent to bringing justice to George Floyd? I am the one who is trying to understand the anomalies here.

Large companies, especially multinationals, have the power and clout to do good. I have worked for three of US multinational companies during my working like since 1996 (I don't get around much). Large firms have thousands of suppliers around the world. When they set high standards for suppliers, especially in third-world countries, improving their employees' welfare is a force for good. I do recall in 2014 when a factory at the Rana Plaza Centre in Dhaka, Bangladesh, collapsed because of the faulty design of the buildings, many workers died. Since then, multinationals have become more stringent with their suppliers on their treatment of workers in third world countries.

I am in danger of veering off course from the topics of injustice and oppression, as seen with Floyd. Still, it was necessary to give preamble into this discourse because I did sense that the anti-Capitalist narrative slipped in when people criticized big businesses (and small) to justify their looting as a way of correcting an injustice on Floyd.

STOP PRESS

After writing the above paragraph, it proved my hunch correct. There is an anti-Capitalist narrative running underneath all the vortex in the same way that blood courses through our veins. I came across an interview with Mark Bray, the author of '*Antifa: The Anti-Fascist Handbook*' and a lecturer at Rutgers University in New Jersey. He said,

> "...*Understand that Capitalism as a system is integral. George Floyd was killed because someone called the police because he had a counterfeit bill allegedly. So, the economic context should not be lost in why he (the Cups Food store) called the police and why he would think of the police as protectors of their economic interests and take such an action. These are inextricably linked, and revolutionaries of (unintelligible) are messy.*"
> (Christiane Amanpour, CNN, 4th June).

There you go. I knew it. The lifelong struggle of Marxist/Socialist/Communist revolutionaries to overthrow Capitalism to protect workers is being manifested by stealth through these anarchists involved in looting and destruction and using Floyd's death tarnish the image of peaceful (and rightfully angry) protestors. Despicable Them.

I have to disagree with Bray because the issue of counterfeit notes has nothing to do with Capitalism. Both free markets and centrally planned economies use the currency. And currency fraud would be a crime in any type of economy. I also disagree with Bray's interpretation of someone from the store calling the police to defend economic interests. They called the police as per protocol regarding counterfeit bills. And what ensued after the police were called should not have happened. The witnesses who observed Floyd's police brutality should have intervened more strongly and made citizens' arrests of these four officers.

We have to go beyond protests and debate and honor the victims of racism and discuss real solutions. Suppose we engage in dialogue and discussion, *inshallah*. In that case, I want to debate the issue of the way forward for improving the lives of people around the world, whether it is addressing racial injustices and economic injustices. Structural changes in policy need to happen and from political and economic standpoints. I would push for Conservative Capitalism as a way forward to propel ALL communities from poverty to prosperity.

CHAPTER 18

INSIGHTS

18. More Personal Insights

As we nearly draw a close to this long letter, let me outline some other insights in the aftermath of Floyd's tragic murder.

18.1 The Three Stages of Anarchy and Terror

The detailed treatment of anarchy and burning of businesses was given above, and you should be convinced by now that it was irresponsible and reprehensible for you to support those who are inciting senseless violence by **woefully using the tragic death of Floyd to promote their anarchy. If you are still not convinced by this, then please read on.**

The trajectory of violence you have supported, which I am still asking you to reflect, retract, and apologize for your explicit support, will inevitably lead to a final destination. The three stages towards that destination are:

Stage 1: You and many of your comrades believe that the critics of violence do not have the right to tell anarchists how to express their rage. Hence there is some justification for attacking and burning down businesses. It is a rage that commemorates George Floyd's death. Some people will then realize that burning of businesses and damage to livelihoods does not equate to Floyd's death; hence, more needs to be done. Enter stage 2.

Stage 2: To achieve a justice other than the legal route, many will try to hurt people and damaging buildings. We have seen the case of Reginald Denny, where after the beating of Rodney King, that those damaging buildings were not enough that some thugs had to beat up a White guy and attempt to murder him. There have been further injuries and loss of life with the protests today because of ensuing violence caused by agitators who want to destroy the powerful messages of peaceful protestors. A 77-year-old retired police officer, David Dorn, was killed, and ten others have died since Floyd's death.

Stage 3: When some more people realize that hurting or injuring someone and burning buildings in revenge for murder is not enough, they would want full equalization, hence retaliate. This means life for a life. Welcome to the terrorist thought process where some White supremacist terrorists and Muslim terrorists kill innocent civilians, thinking it would justify killing their own people. The thought process is warped, and I have been obvious what the Islamic position is on protecting civilians even during wartime; I am sure you will agree to this. Yes, I know. You will automatically divert to the bombing of civilians in Iraq by the Western military or bombing of Palestinians. I am putting a scratch on this record of automatic/autonomic scripted response and bringing you back. We have standards to uphold, even if we may not like them. They came from our Creator. Period. So, when you justify the burning and looting as justifiable anger '**by any means necessary**,' this is a launching pad, a conveyor belt, and a one-directional journey from the destruction of buildings to the destruction of innocent life. There are no brakes, no service stops, no bumps along the road towards the final destination of unjustifiable anger through terrorism. **Stage 1 WILL lead to Stage 3.** What are your thoughts on the Iranian Parliament where its lawmaker encouraged all the parliamentarians to chant '**Death to America**' in the usual fist-pumping gestures, response to George Floyd's murder? A convenient diversion from their killing of over 1,000 protestors against the Iranian Government. The question I just asked is not rhetorical. I would be grateful for an answer.

18.2. Protect Vs Protest: Turbocharging Coronavirus.

I have heard from a conservative (not politically but in outlook) think tank here in the UK, the Henry Jackson Society, that the far right were weaponizing the COVID epidemic by blaming the Jews for creating it and spreading it to make profits on a vaccine that they were going to come up with. COVID is being used to propel their antisemitism. This is worrying.

A further insight I have relating to COVID and the mass protests taking place is this. Although the mainstream media touched on this, it was only factual but did not draw implications. The COVID pandemic has taught scientists that there is a disproportionate casualty rate for the BAME (Black, Asian, and Minority Ethnic) community. The likely cause is because of comorbidities that we have. The virus originated from a wet market in Wuhan, China, and spread rapidly throughout the world. BAME casualty rates are high.

Recall what I said above that the agitators and criminals hiding behind the peaceful protestors are using Floyd's death to break communities by breaking businesses and causing anarchy? I said that the White folks who had been involved in this agitation could be either from the far right/White Supremacy movement, or they could be White Liberals from Antifa. Or maybe both? I don't know. But one thing is for sure. Recall in history how White racists lynched Blacks and burnt their buildings before the civil rights movement took hold. The Tulsa Massacre in 1921 is a case in point. White residents went on a rampage and killed Black families and attacked Black-owned businesses.

Now, if White supremacists are behind the recent anarchy, we have seen, what would be their end game? Yes, they would target shops and businesses as they did in the Tulsa massacre to destroy Black folks' livelihoods. A very crude way of ascertaining whether White supremacists are behind this is to identify a correlation between the anarchy/looting locations and the prevalence of Black residents, which these businesses support and offer their services to. White supremacy inspired anarchy is likely to take place in higher concentrations of Black or BAME residents. If there is a significant correlation, it indicates that the dark forces of anarchy may well be triggered by White supremacists to deprive the BAME communities of livelihoods and economic support.

But this is not the only end game. Destroying businesses would not be enough. They would want more BAME people killed. In the absence of lynching and burning at the cross, what is the alternative method of killing them?

Weaponization of the COVID virus. What appeared because of unhygienic conditions in a wet market in Wuhan can now be weaponized on their soil, where the spread of the virus has been alarming, taking casualties on its journey. Knowing the higher fatality rate of BAME victims, what better way to unleash this biological fury by engineering fury so that the BAME communities take the bait and come out in droves, thus reversing the decline in the infection rates and death rates as lockdown is locked down and people are gathering en masse. How would they engineer emotions and harness crowd psychology? They may infiltrate.

I don't have evidence to prove my point, and I rarely cite an opinion without evidence. If White supremacists are behind this, then what we are witnessing makes perfect sense. The death of Floyd wasn't enough. Lay the bait, get the BAME communities out in rage, and infect more.

A further insight I have relating to COVID is this. COVID infection rates will rise. When it does, and more BAME communities are infected, and death rates increase, for what reason did the doctors and nurses risk their lives, and some of them sacrificed their lives on the front line so we could stay indoors and protect ourselves and our families? Time and time again, we were told by doctors and nurses in the British health service known as the National Health Service (NHS) to stay at home and not risk our health and our lives so they could carry out the work to help patients already infected.

I don't know about the US, but there is a disproportionate number of deaths amongst doctors and nurses from BAME backgrounds here in the UK. As mentioned before, the virus causes a higher fatality rate amongst our BAME communities because we have higher comorbidities. As lockdown goes into freefall, what was the point of sacrificing their lives to protect us if we will not listen and risk more infections and fatalities, especially amongst the BAME communities? Healthcare professionals who died on the front lines trying to save patient's lives DIED IN VAIN because protesters are doing the opposite of what they were asked to do by them. Not the protesters' fault, I blame the sinister forces (maybe White Supremacists or otherwise) who are agitators and have encouraged people to come out in droves during the pandemic. In summary:

As COVID spreads and affects more BAME communities, sinister forces are being turbocharged to affect more BAME groups as they come out in droves.

These agitators insult George Floyd and his family by using his death to destroy businesses (Floyd's family never permitted to do this on his behalf), thus affecting the economic support that business owners and their communities rely on. I would not be surprised if the Black/BAME communities have been adversely affected by this vandalism and looting -- a 2020 version of Tulsa 1921. They, too, are insulting the dead doctors and nurses by coaxing mass crowds to come out en masse.

If I am wrong about this and White supremacists are not triggering the violence, but White liberals from Antifa (or Socialists/Marxists) are, then what is their endgame? The endgame of Marxists is the overthrow of Capitalism, and they will use any opportunity to engineer an uprising. Mass protests are being staged worldwide in parallel reflects the left's/Socialists'/Marxists' organizational capabilities. But why would they urge people, especially BAME communities, to come out knowing that their health will be at further risk? I don't know. I hope to God that I am wrong about all of this and that herd immunity kicks in. DON'T

TAKE THE BAIT and risk the health and wellbeing of you and your families during the pandemic.

Sister Linda, can you see what is going on here? Do you want to be part of the problem by supporting violence and also mass protests that could increase health risk and risk to life? Or do you want to be part of the solution?

It is down to the FBI and CIA to find out that behind the agitation and instigation, I am sure the UK will be happy to help and send over MI6 at Her Majesty's pleasure.

18.3 BAME Achievements - A History of Silence

They have taught us in schools about the British Empire and its positive and negative elements. We all know about the institution of African slavery and colonization and India's administration under British rule. And the ensuing fight for independence, although it wasn't a fight at all, Mahatma Gandhi is one of the very few leaders who took a non-violent approach and won. We all know this history of subjugation and independence. Why aren't we taught in parallel to India's contribution and the Hindus made to the world before? The outstanding achievements they made in astronomy and mathematics? Or the contributions that the Muslim Moghal dynasty made? Today, India is being resurrected, and poverty is declining. They send missions to the Moon and Mars (Mission Mangalayaan cost only a fraction of NASA's spending on similar missions). This Hindu country promoted minorities to the top. They had a Muslim President, Abdul Kalam, who led the Indian space program and nuclear program. And they had a Sikh Prime Minister, Manmohan Singh. Before you divert again, let me take a step ahead of you and acknowledge that there is a problem with the caste system and recent communal tensions. But India is heading in the right direction. Indian millionaires and billionaires are buying up British companies. Some Indians are getting into the upper echelons of British governance. They are too busy outperforming and outdoing their previous masters to worry about revenge against British establishments. Do you, Sister Linda, believe that they should have exerted fire and fury upon the British after independence, or do you agree with the route towards privileged status that they are pursuing and even outperforming in some areas compared to the White communities the UK?

George Floyd's death and ensuing peaceful protests have highlighted systemic racism that needs to be abolished. It is encouraging to see those White folks say that they need to listen more, and they can no longer take their way of life for granted, now that they know that their fellow ethnic neighbors may have differing experiences. They teach us in history about slavery in America and the fight for freedom and ensuing racism that continued even after Blacks were freed from slavery. They should teach everyone this, and I hope they are in their school curriculum. However, as with the Indian example above, there is an eerie silence of Black communities' achievements. Have we heard of the following names? Hiram Revels, John Lynch, Lloyd Hall, Garrett Morgan, Patricia Bath, Elijah McCoy, Granville Woods, Thomas Jennings, Marie Van Brown, Dorothy Vaughan, Mary Jackson, Katherine Johnson, Frederick McKinley, Guion Bluford, Charles Bolden, Mae Jemison, Stephanie Wilson…. and the list goes on. If you and other readers of this letter need to do a Google search on most of these names, we have a severe problem. Why didn't we know these names? Some Black entrepreneurs are millionaires and billionaires. Why don't we know about them and model their successes? They may be smaller than White folks, but they are there and have proven that the glass ceiling can be broken.

How many of us knew that Timbuktu in Mali, Africa, was a learning center under the Songhai empire in the 12th century? How many of us knew that surgery's medical techniques came from Africa or that vaccination came from Africa (very topical today, as there is a race against time to find a vaccine for COVID-19). How many know that the Dogon tribe in Mali was aware of the Dog Star, Sirius, is part of a binary star system (Sirius A and Sirius B) long before European astronomers discovered this through the telescope?

I came across a very bizarre hidden racism, which I think has been missed by historians, is building the pyramids in Egypt. European archaeologists were baffled by the construction of the pyramids without the use of modern equipment. They did eventually discover the secret only very recently; within the last ten years, I believe. But before that, this was an enigma for hundreds of years, so much so that some UFO enthusiasts hypothesized that the pyramids were built with the help of alien technology! It did not occur to the archaeologists that Egypt's Black civilization had the know-how and ingenuity to build complicated structures that baffled Europeans for a long time. Remember our friend, whom I mentioned earlier, who thought Africa had not developed technologically because of the hot weather? We should be laughing out loud now.

I haven't mentioned the advances in science, mathematics, and medicine that Muslims and Arabs made that triggered the European Renaissance hundreds of years ago. We can at least agree on this, so no need to delve into this further, but it makes sense for non-Muslim readers of this letter to avail themselves of this part of Islamic history and do some research.

Which group does it serve when we are taught ONLY about the struggles of the past and present, the slavery, segregation, racism, lynching, burning on the cross, etc. but are clueless when it comes to successes and achievements of successful BAME high achievers? The group which would like to see the BAME psyche aggressively crushed down to a state of perpetual suffering, underachievement, victimization so that we think that we will never reach the holy grail of White privilege. Once we are down there, then it is easier to control us.

What affected me after the death of Floyd and ensuing protests was the case of Simone, a Black five-year-old girl in Houston, Texas. She was out with her parents on a protest march. She cried and asked a police officer if he was going to kill her. The policeman gave her a big hug. I was close to tears when I read this story. The day after I heard about this story, I cried, but it was in my dream. It was a place of safety to let myself go compared to my waking state. My external persona exhibits the British stiff upper lip HOW DARE people give Simone the impression that her life will end quickly in a policeman's hands. Why hasn't she been told that she can become another Dorothy Vaughan or Mae Jemison or Barack Obama? This is latent child abuse.

When President Obama responded to the riots, he emphasized the message of hope…. that there is hope. Of course, there is. Let's focus on that. Likewise, the Duchess of Cambridge, Megan Markle, told children in her old school in LA, *"I'm sorry. I'm so sorry that you have to grow up in a world where this is still present." "That's something you should have an understanding of, but an understanding of as a history lesson, not as your reality."*

This is it. How do we ensure now that this is not their reality or their future? We can all agree that structural changes need to be structural to eliminate systemic racism and other forms of discrimination that I have described elsewhere. Structural changes start with changing the structure of our mindset. We should no longer allow ourselves to be dictated that our lives will always be in a state of perpetual wretchedness and victimization. That privilege/success/opportunity can never come our way. They are coming. The Indian/South Asian and African communities are breaking through, and many are outperforming White folks, thus reaching Mount Privilege. Do you or the British readers of this letter know that Black children from Africa are outperforming White kids in school? If not, why not? Other communities, Native Indians, Latinos, Aborigines, etc. can break through and have broken through. As we have seen, Black history is replete with achievements, and they should be our inspiration too.

Last point on this. Recall I mentioned earlier about Rev. Al Sharpton's inspiring eulogy of George Floyd. I agree with almost all of what he said, with one exception. If I understood him correctly, he said that if George Floyd had been a polished bourgeoise brother, they (i.e., the Black masses) would not have had value, but because Floyd was from them, they were valued. If I heard him correctly, he is the crux of the problem I have been talking about. What is it about Black success and achievement that makes them different from the Black masses? Why consider Black millionaires as others when they should be examples of inspiration because this is what we should ALL be aiming for… that mountain called privilege/success/achievement?

18.4. *Black/Asian Conformity and Latent Racism.* Where did the idea come from that certain groups must conform to individual thinking or way, and if they don't, they are sell-outs? This is stems from the far left/Socialist view of collective thinking. Here we see the Marxist/Socialist values and Capitalist/Conservative values at loggerheads here. Collective, restricted and homogenous thinking versus

Individual breakthrough free thought. This explains why commentators on the left who see ethnic politicians join Conservative politics have a problem. These Black/Asian individuals are not conforming.

I came across two such left-wing commentators. One was Kehinde Andrews of the UK's newspaper, The Guardian. He was commenting on Prime Minister Boris Johnson and the fact that he had selected a diverse cabinet. I am no fan of Boris Johnson, and I was surprised (a pleasant one) when he chose a diverse cabinet. Kehinde warns the readers not to be fooled by this diversity because the ethnic Ministers are very right wing. You don't see the latent racism here? I see it. The left narrative must conform to the left's way of thinking because of their ethnicity. That there is diversity in the current Conservative cabinet is dismissed because they hold 'wrong' philosophies based on their ethnicities. When we are told that we must think a certain way because of our skin color, what do you call this if not racism? Compare this with White folks who venture into various types of politics, whether it is the left or the right. In the UK, we have significant parties: Conservatives, Labour, Liberal Democrats, UK Independence Party, and the Green Party.
You will see White members and activists in all of them. No one lectures to them. They don't have to think in a certain way because of their skin color. They are free to think, ponder, question and debate, and no one gives a damn if there is a diversity of thinking among them. But when Blacks and other BAME members break out of the left's thought process and think freely, and some decide to join Conservativism, they are sell-outs and '*tut-tut naughty*!' There is a lot of thought and discussion about diversity and inclusion. But that is only in name and a defunct slogan unless there is a diversity of free thought and opinions within our BAME communities.

DIVERSITY DOES NOT MEAN DIVISION.

DIVERSITY DOES NOT MEAN DIVISIVENESS.

UNITY IN DIVERSITY IS THE GOAL.

The second commentator I came across is Afua Hirsch, another columnist for the Guardian. She commented on the appointment of a Black/Nigerian Conservative MP, Kemi Badenoch, to Equalities Minister, and she is also Under-Secretary to the Treasury. Afua criticizes Kemi for holding different views. Hence her appointment as a Minister should not be taken seriously. There you go again, Badenoch is not conforming; therefore, she is dismissed. You still don't see the latent racism here?

Back to Kehinde Andrews. In the same article mentioned above, he criticized Condoleezza Rice, the ex-Secretary of State under President George W. Bush. He stated that when Hurricane Katrina unleashed its fury in 2006, she was still on holiday buying shoes. This is factually correct but the wrong interpretation. Kehinde provided the link to this story. The story was straightforward: Rice spoke with Michael Chertoff, the then-Secretary of Homeland Security, and asked whether she could assist. He did not need her help at the time, so she continued her holiday. When it turned out that the devastation of Katrina was worse than predicted, she told President Bush that she was coming back, and she did. What Kehinde missed was that Condoleezza Rice called herself out for her mistake in not coming back earlier. That's what outstanding leaders do. They acknowledge their mistakes and take ownership of them (something which you have failed to do, Sister Linda). Kehinde overlooked this and overlooked her accomplishments.

Instead, she just focused on her mistake because she is a Black Republican. He also dismissed the British-Pakistani, Sajid Javid, the Home Secretary under Prime Minister Theresa May. Javid decided to strip away the British citizenship of Shamima Begum in 2019. She had initially run away from home in London and joined ISIS and married an ISIS fighter. When ISIS was defeated, she wanted to come back to the creature comforts of the British way of life. There was controversy about this in the UK, and I spoke on national radio to support Sajid Javid's decision. Again, this brown Pakistani-British man did not conform to what is expected by the left. Hence, he has no value as an ethnic Conservative Home Secretary by left-wing columnists.

I wonder how these columnists would view the British-Ghanaian Conservative MP, Kwasi Kwarteng? He is a Minister. I look up to him as an excellent example to follow. He achieved first-class grades in two degrees he undertook at Cambridge University and also studied and Harvard University. You can imagine what they will say. They will find faults with him because he does not conform the way they want him to serve. They will probably charge him for being too right wing.

The bottom line is this. If you are BAME, then you have to conform to a specific ideology because of your color. If you differ, then you no longer represent the BAME community; you are mere tokens. But if you are White, you can have a diversity of opinions, and you will NEVER hear the phrase, *'token Whites.'* Work that one out. I know that you and your comrades of the left have never thought of this before.

18.5. All Lives Should Matter

This was touched on before, and here is the elaboration. I agree with the statement which I have often seen bandied around, '***All Lives Matter.***' It looks at Mankind homogenous unit. But a valid criticism of this statement is that it doesn't reflect the disparities between various cultures and ethnicities and assumes that all lives are being treated equally well. They are not. EVERYONE should support the slogan **Black Lives Matter** and become an ally. Black Lives Matter is not asking for special treatment; it asks for something that everyone else is asking for, which is to be perceived and treated equally. They are not excluding anyone else; they focus on Black lives and injustices as a starting point.

Instead of using the term, '**All Lives Matter**.' I prefer the moto, '***All Lives Should Matter.***' This will reflect the current situation and accommodate disparities and the aspiration to close the gaps wherever they are so that all lives reach that state of equality of opportunity and prosperity. There are systemic racial issues now, and once resolved, we all go to that place called success and privilege. More on privilege later.

18.6. Defund or Reform the Police? Please Learn from the Muslims

There has been a lot of talk about defunding the police forces in the US. I understand this to mean to reduce the police's powers or break them up and be replaced by... ***errrrrm* who**?

Who are you going to call if a crime is taking place, Sister Linda? In one of your Facebook posts, you support the defunding of police everywhere in the US. And on 1st June, you posted the following sentence, '***Arrest ALL the cops.***' I have to marvel at the poor choice of words and the emotional imbalance you display now and again. This is not ad hominem. I don't do ad hominem. The reason for stating this is that your words carry powerful meaning, and you have the ear of millions of people. If your comments cannot be unifying and inclusive, then this will have negative implications. The worst of which we witnessed when you supported the looting and anarchy as expressions of legitimate anger, which inadvertently ended up with death threats against the Palestinian owner of Cups Food store…the trigger point of the sequence of events that led to the murder of George Floyd. If a fatality had taken place within that Palestinian family due to this 'justifiable anger,' you would have been culpable. You realized this and offered a magnificent defense of the Cups Food Store to mitigate threats that the owner had been receiving.

You and your comrades supported the defunding of police and treat ALL police officers as murderers and criminals. Two things are happening here.

First, many police officers call in sick because of the negative images people have of them, police resources are being stretched. It was painful to hear the words Chief of Police in Seattle, Carmen Best, and the Acting Chief of Police in Atlanta, Rodney Bryant. They said that they were having difficulties in responding to calls on time. If crime rates and rapes increase because of defunding police, you and your comrades will be culpable.

Second, you are unconsciously setting up the Muslim communities for a backlash by Islamophobes. When you imply that ALL police officers are responsible for a minority of corrupt officers' evil deeds, you are giving ammunition to Islamophobes. The latter blame ALL Muslims for the dishonest acts of terrorism by a minority of extremists. You and I have tried very hard to convey the message in the media that not all Muslims are terrorists, although many terrorists are Muslims (let's not forget White supremacy terrorists), hence people should not judge all Muslims by some evil suicide bombers. You know this. Yet you are foisting Islamophobia's equivalence on the US Police forces by blaming all of them for a minority of corrupt officers.

DO YOU NOT SEE THE CONTRADICTION HERE?

18.7. Cooper Vs Cooper – The White Liberal Liar and the Cool Black Bird Watcher

Meet the Coopers. They are not a couple. They were strangers who had an interaction in Central Park in New York City. Amy Cooper is a White woman walking her dog in Central Park, and Christian Cooper is a Black man who was bird watching. You know the story, but I am recounting this for the benefit of readers outside the US. Christian told the woman to put her dog on the leash. She didn't like being lectured to by a Black man, so she then called the police and stated that he was threatening her life, thus potentiating the stereotype of a typical 'violent' Black man about to attack her. She thought she would get a rapid response from the police. Christian caught this interchange on his mobile phone camera.

I suspect that you (Sister Linda) and I will have a different interpretation of this incident. We agree that Amy was a racist and deserved to be fired. She also deserves to be arrested for racism and falsely accusing Christian of attempted murder. We agree on this. Who is the victim here? Knowing the Socialist/liberal/Marxist way of thinking, the Black guy, Christian Cooper, is the victim. As discussed above, you and your Socialist comrades' mindset is that the Black communities are in perpetual states of victimization and wretchedness. You never see them as achievers and winners. During the moment of the exchange, the Black guy was a victim of racism and false allegations. If you watch the video, you cannot help but notice how calm and smooth

Christian Cooper was, then the very unsophisticated and uncouth Amy Cooper. He came out as the better person, a more superior person. She came out of it as a victim of her lies and falsities. White privilege failed her. She was eventually fired from her workplace—good riddance to bad rubbish. Christian Cooper is the winner here, and Amy Cooper is the loser.

Now, do you see the Black guy in a different light? Or do you still see him as a permanent victim, a loser, and a very beaten man? I am trying to shift your thinking and perception, which is the starting point of any paradigm shift we will bring about in society.

18.8. Lauren vs. Hasan

In the introductory part of my letter, I stated briefly that I had a fallout (which is very rare, I always end on good terms with my interlocutors) with a left-wing White Socialist woman here in the UK. In one of her Facebook posts, she slated the UK Conservative Government's policies during the lockdown, and her position was going viral. I responded in kind with a point-by-point rebuttal. I have a habit of providing detailed responses and did so in Lauren's case. Instead of debating with me or engaging in dialogue, she told me to take down my post; otherwise, she would launch litigation against me for harassment. Harassment is a crime anywhere in the world.

Why did she claim harassment? Because in my response, I advised the readers to read Lauren's post first to understand her views and then read my response. The reader could then make a fair judgment. Her understanding was that I was trying to direct people to her post to harass her. Luckily, a few good people wrote to me, stating that there was no call for harassment and that I was polite throughout my responses. I refuse to take down my post, and it is still up. However, this got me thinking.

Why would she be so reactive and emotional about the whole thing, given that my response was not going viral compared to hers? What was so threatening about it? From my experience with the left and Socialists, they expect BAME communities to think like them and vote for their parties (Labour Party in the UK). If BAME people believe differently and veer towards the Conservative side, then they are coconuts or sell-outs. Because I am a brown guy who bleeds blue, she did not expect me to prove her wrong. And when she had to deal with the fact that a brown Conservative man had responded to her, well, she couldn't deal with it because this is not how a BAME person should behave. There were underlying racist factors at play here. Just as many on the right are in denial about systemic or institutional racism, there are those on the left who are in denial about their underlying racism when dealing with BAME people who disagree with their views.

When the incident between Amy Cooper and Christian Cooper took place, it reminded me of my experience, which I mentioned above. There is a parallel here, although their case is more serious. In their case, a White liberal woman didn't like being corrected by a Black man, so she falsely accused him of attempted murder. In my case, a White Socialist woman did not like being corrected by a brown man is on the 'wrong' side of the political fence, hence sought to threaten litigation based on a false charge of harassment. Note well. **White folks who are political activists on the left dislike to be lectured by BAME people who disagree with them**. This is not just a statement I drew out of thin air. **I am issuing a gentle challenge to prove me wrong**.

18.9. Anti-Capitalism Strikes Back

In section *17.8.4* above, I mentioned that there seemed to be an underlying anti-Capitalist narrative at play here based on what I understood from your speeches and posts, which was further evidenced by a comment from Mark Bray of Rutgers University where he stated on CNN that the police were there to defend the Capitalist economics. Since writing that, further evidence has been brought to the light of this anti-Capitalist narrative. A recent documentary, entitled, '*8 mins 46 secs*,' was produced the British channel, Sky TV. It dealt with the tragedy of Floyd's murder and the ensuing protests by Black Lives Matter. Zellie Imani of BLM stated that the power structures needed to be destroyed. He commented that President Obama and other Black officials who reached the state of power didn't affect the Black masses' lives. Hence these power structures that control us should be dismantled. Furthermore, he stated that the ladders that people climb up to reach power positions should be knocked down (Timestamp: 34 mins onward).

I mentioned the Guardian columnist, Kehinde Andrews, in section *18.4* above. You recall that he didn't think much of BAME people who occupied the corridors of power within the Conservative Prime Minister Boris Johnson's Cabinet and Ministerial team. In the Sky documentary, Andrews stated that the only way to eliminate racism is to destroy the political economy (timestamp: 40 mins). What does this mean? The political economies in the Western world where protests are taking place are Capitalist economies. That is why the anarchists (whom you support) are using the death of George Floyd to drown out the pertinent messages of peaceful protestors to trigger global unrest and overthrow Capitalist systems. The Cold War had ended after the collapse of the Berlin Wall in 1989 and the Soviet Union's subsequent fall. It ended, but what has continued is the

'Latent War' (I have just invented this phrase) against traditional norms, values, religion, and Capitalism.

The choice is straightforward, and I will use the 'ladder' analogy that Zellie Imani used when he stated that the ladders should be taken away from people. Socialism and anarchists want to take out the ladders from the few people who have them to make everyone equal… what this means is equally poor. Capitalism wants to give the ladder of opportunity to everyone so that they can have equal opportunities to climb up, reach Mount Privilege, thrive, and give back to society. Here is the irony. White folks predominantly occupied the power structures created by opportunities and privilege. Still, now that the BAME people are climbing the ladders of hope towards privilege status, Socialists and the left seek to take away these ladders and refuse to recognize the significant successes that BAME groups have made. Instead, they will ostracise these BAME groups if they hold different views to the left's outrage narrative. As people come out of poverty and raise the ladders of opportunities and successes, and when we reach the peak of Mount Privilege, everyone will be prosperous. There will be no more angry left, which means there will be no room for Socialism. The image of itself that Socialism is printing on the world will cease to exist. Socialism is staring at its own mortality.

CHAPTER 19

EXPERIMENTING WITH RACISM

19. Thought Experiments

19.1. How Racist are You? (I am directing this to other readers who are reading this).

About a week ago, a group of passionate Black men who wore scarves to hide their faces. They circled and wrapped a White policeman. There was no gap for exit nor entry.

What picture comes to mind? What do you think would happen, and why? These Black men surrounded a police officer to PROTECT him because he became detached from his legion. If you thought they were going to attack him in revenge, please call yourself out for unconscious bias racist thinking. How dare we think because these men were Black

102

and wearing scarves that they were going to attack the White policeman? Why didn't it occur to you they are the ones who would do the protection thing of the lone policeman? Do you think they did the right thing to protect him? If not, then you would think they were Black sell-outs. In which case, welcome to the second form of racism you hold, those Black men should behave in a certain way, and if they don't conform to your world view, they are sell-outs.

19.2. Let's Talk About Privilege

What is privilege? I understand this to mean achieving success in material wealth and emotional/spiritual well-being because of the provided opportunities.

Is privilege static or fluid? I believe it is fluid. Others will think that it is static if it is White privilege.

What is White privilege? Here is a quote from Wikipedia:

> *Peggy McIntosh describes the advantages that Whites in Western societies enjoy and non-Whites do not experience, as "an invisible package of unearned assets" White privilege denotes both obvious and less obvious passive advantages that White people may not recognize they have, which distinguishes it from overt bias or prejudice. These include cultural affirmations of one's worth, presumed greater social status, and freedom to move, buy, work, play, and speak freely. The effects can be seen in professional, educational, and personal contexts. The concept of White privilege also implies the right to assume the universality of one's own experiences, marking others as different or exceptional while perceiving oneself as usual.*

I understand this definition to mean that White people will have an advantage over non-Whites when presented with similar opportunities. And this may be based on past European colonialism. It is difficult to say whether past European colonialism directly impacts the options we have today. If there were a direct link between historical colonialism and present-day opportunities, we would have a concept of 'Muslim or Arab privilege.' We don't hear this phrase.

As mentioned briefly earlier, Arabs/Muslims conquered other empires and made advances in science, technology, and medicine. Some of it was a transfer of knowledge from the Hindus, the Chinese, and Greeks. Other advances were organic (from within the Muslim civilization) and when Europe was considered in the Dark Ages. So, there must have been a concept of *'Arab or Muslim privilege'* at the time (I know some non-Muslims will talk about *Dhimmitude*...that is different and another topic) over their White European neighbors.

I have not come across this, but if it were the case, then we would still see privileged Muslim status today over and above Europeans because of past Muslim conquests or colonization. But you and I would argue that the Muslim empire collapsed under its weight and complacency; hence its effects would not be seen today, and we should not expect *'Muslim privilege'* to filter through. So, why do you expect White/European privilege to filter through to today even after the collapse of European colonialism and the abolition of slavery? (I know about South Africa and that Apartheid ended only recently. For now, I am sticking with America and Europe).

Racism still exists, and that is undeniable (those who deny it has some learning to do), and I have explained racism against BAME communities above, as well as other forms of discrimination we see across the world. I do welcome the statements by many White folks that they should listen more. It is only by sharing the different experiences that we understand each other better.

As mentioned before, there are no no-go areas for racism. And I also said that BAME communities are breaking through the glass ceiling and bettering their lives towards reaching the state of privilege in the way I defined it, i.e., material success, happiness, spiritual wellbeing, and securing bright futures for their children. There is some way to go before the gap is closed. But I see a breakthrough. You are not. Why? More importantly, there have been breakthroughs in the past by BAME communities. Still, that part of history is surreptitiously silent. We are programmed to believe that only White communities achieved the highest levels of privilege, success, and influence and that it would remain that way in perpetuity.

That thought experiment. I am coming to it. The above preamble leads nicely to it, so here it is:

Example 1: Imagine you have a White millionaire and a BAME working-class person. Who is privileged? The White dude. Both of us would race to say this first. Now suppose that you have a BAME millionaire and a White working-class person. Who is privileged? Who is successful? (Let's ignore the happiness index, for now, let's assume that when someone is more prosperous, they would be happier because the future is secure for the next generation; but not all rich people are so glad though). What would you and your comrades on the left say? You may still think the White guy is privileged. Why? Because he is White? Suppose his circumstances are such that he has fewer opportunities for a good education, employment, and entrepreneurship than the

BAME person who used these opportunities. What is it about the Whiteness that propels him to that holy grail status of privilege vs. the BAME guy? If it is past European colonialism, then I refer you back to the discussion above about Muslim/Arab privilege, which has not filtered through. Suppose the White skin color alone gives the working-class man his privileged status, even though he did not use the opportunities provided to him. How is this different from White superiority? White privilege = White supremacy. That seems to the subconscious thought at play here.

I believe that the gaps in prosperity between White communities and BAME communities can and will close. The process has started and is **unstoppable**.

Example 2. Indians (South Asians), Chinese communities, and African communities are staring to outperform some White communities in education, business, and influence. Who is privileged or prosperous? I say the BAME groups. What say you, and why?

What the above two examples are showing is that privilege is not static; it is fluid. You may have a picture of different layers of privilege, with Blacks occupying the bottom and Whites at the top. There may even be various permutations and combinations in between depending on sub-races, gender differentiation, and so on. Do you believe that one day the opportunities for prosperity can avail itself to them and that the layers would be reconfigured to be a flat shape instead of a pyramid? I believe it can happen and is happening. Why don't you? Yes, big shit is happening. We can all see that. So, are good things, but they only appear in your blind spot.

Example 3. My community is the Bangladeshi community. In the 70s, there were problems with racism (as with other Asian and Black communities) in the UK. In the 1990s, I remember the racist attack on a Bengali boy, Quddus Ali, in East London. He was 17 at the time and had the ambition to become a policeman. He was set upon by a racist White gang known as the 'National Front.' Six men and one woman beat him to unconsciousness. He became disabled after that incident. Afterward, 7,000 Bengalis marched to Downing Street (where the Prime Minister works and resides) demanding change in-laws. Later on, the Socialists intervened, and there were protests and strikes. This incidence of a racist attack on Ali defined the Bengali community.

Over a decade later, I visited that part of London for political campaigning, and I noticed that there were some improvements within the community thanks to regeneration. I was still concerned with the number of people from my community who lived in council or social housing. During the Candidates Hustings, I made a point that I wanted to see how we could provide opportunities for people to get out of social housing and into the private property so they could increase their wealth and provide better opportunities for the next generation. It is not the language you would hear amongst Socialists. Another decade later, the Bengali community is prospering. Racist attacks by the National Front no longer define us, and while racism still exists, I see prosperity. I am seeing Bengali millionaires who have made it here in the UK, unheard of 30 years ago. I want to see the gaps close and more prosperity among my community and ALL communities, including poor White working-class communities.

What would happen if most of my Bengali community in 20 years become prosperous, wealthy, securing bright futures for the next generation and giving back to society? How would your fellow Socialist and Marxist comrades react? What will be the place of Socialism then? It would stare at its mortality. I gained an insight into the Socialist mindset on prosperity in 2004 on national radio. I asked a left-wing candidate for the London Mayoral elections, Lindsey German, what policies she would implement to ensure more impoverished people or working class could better themselves. She said, *"they don't want to better themselves. They are happy where they are."* There you have it. In reality, it is Socialists and Marxists who don't want poor people to better themselves. Socialism/Marxism needs poor people to remain poor and angry because it can exercise control.

19.3. Africa Rising

I don't know if this is a thought experiment, but I have put this example here because I am asking you to think. Although I am from Bangladesh and belong to the South Asian group, I've had a soft spot for Africa after visiting Nigeria and South Africa two decades ago. While we consider America and Russia being superpowers today, China and India are considered the next superpowers in 50 years. It is useful when third world countries are catching up. Karl Marx never dreamed of this. Have you ever thought Africa will one day become a superpower? If not, why not?

If you haven't, it doesn't make you a racist. Still, it reinforces the stereotypes that you and your comrades have: today's entire Black community is victims of past slavery, beatings, brutality, racism, underachievement, and will stay that way. You ignore Black achievements which further accentuates this reinforcement. That is why it would not have occurred to you and your supporters that Africa will become a superpower one day and lead the world. If I am correct in my understanding of your thought process, then maybe it is worth reflecting on your world view as it quakes because of a fundamental change that is hopefully taking place.

Conversely, the reinforcement of stereotypes among the White supremacists and the far right Blacks are underachievers because they have a low IQ and are inclined to violence. Both groups have negative stereotypes about Black communities for different reasons. They are both wrong.

19.4. One Word That Will Turn Away Millions

That one word is '**ALL.**' This is an unfortunate fact. Here is the thought experiment. It is difficult to estimate how many people came out to protest (leave aside the violent ones) worldwide over the last two weeks. Let's say a ballpark figure of 3 million people give or take. They and most of us are allies of the '*Black Lives Matter*' movement. Now (as alluded to earlier), change the slogan to '*ALL Black Lives Matter,*' which includes unborn Black babies who would be otherwise aborted. What do you think is going to happen? Watch closely how over 2 million people would look to the ground, turn around and walk away and go back to their homes. COVID-19 could not keep them away despite the risks to health and life, and despite doctors and nurses who sacrificed their lives to protect theirs. But mention this group of forgotten Black lives, and watch them go home at light speed because of this one word. You said rightly in one of your videos that White people should have candid conversations with their families and the older generations about racism and how it affects Black Lives. All families, regardless of race, should discuss these. But would they be candid enough and brave enough to talk about another loss of life that is taking place? The dinner tables would fall silent.

Do you see the massive contradiction here? Your sense of justice and calling out injustice *'wherever it is'* are mere slogans unless acted upon with consistency. Let us have a candid discussion on this issue if we engage in dialogue. Abortion affects unborn babies from all races globally. I get a sense that you are not too concerned about White lives. So, let's stick to Black lives. Please explain why the lives of Black unborn babies do not matter.

Abortion is a dark stain on humanity, and I call out our fellow Muslims for their deafening silence. We are useless for correcting this injustice even though many are happy to demonstrate outside Israeli embassies or get involved in Stop the War coalitions. I refer you to your Facebook post on 4th June where you said,

> *"Please, Allah, be the shield we need at this moment. I cry to you, don't let us lose any more unjustly. Please make the movements for justice successful. Please, Allah, we will do what we can with the blessings you have given us, but our trust is in YOU. Please, Allah."*

A perfect prayer, and this brother is raising his hands with you. May Allah answer your prayers. I need not say anything more about this because you know where this is going. It falls upon fellow Christians and Catholics who have been at the forefront of the campaign to protect the unborn lives. May Allah blesse them and grants them victory as the rest of our Muslim communities continue our observations as bystanders.

CHAPTER 20

WHO ARE WE?

20. Conclusion

Review the above, Sister Linda. You and I follow the same Quran and Sunnah (way of the Prophet), and our concept of human rights should converge and should be similar. But we are divergent in our idea of human rights. Maybe your gravitation to the left of politics has landed you in a cognitive dissonant situation where you are trying to resolve or overlook a cocktail of contradictions of values and invoking a masterful use of diversion and pivoting when someone exposes your contradiction or makes a criticism. And I have landed on the right-wing of politics, and I can say with certainty that there is a convergence for religion and right-wing politics. It doesn't mean that all right-wing people are religious, and they don't have a monopoly on faith. Some are

Atheists, like Ayaan Hirsi Ali and Douglas Murray. I recognize that Christianity had been used in the past to justify slavery and to justify its abolition. Today there is a narrative among the far right that they want to preserve a White Christian Europe. I recognize these, and I deal with this in a video I responded to the far right (which is mentioned below). But the general point I made above still stands.

It doesn't mean that there are no religious people on the left. There are. President Obama did quote from the Bible a few times, which was nice to hear given the secularist onslaught against religion. But religious people of the far left need to confront and resolve the conflicts between their left-wing/Socialist/Marxist ideologies based on an internal moral compass where the needle is spinning at warp speed, and their religious views. It is a conflict hard to resolve, and it is a mountain hard to climb.

My above letter may give the impression that I have a gripe with Socialism and the left. Well, I do, but I had invested more time responding to the far right and White Supremacy after the New Zealand attacks when I did a 3-hr video. The link is here:

https://youtu.be/2a-piFzrceU

With unwavering certainty, I can say that this is the ONLY detailed response to the White supremacy terrorist New Zealand attacker, Brenton Tarrant's Replacement Manifesto, that you will find on the internet. I also responded to arguments raised by non-violent White rights activists. The video reached nearly half a million people on Facebook, about 2,000 watched it, and only one person responded and engaged in dialogue. Unfortunately, his contribution wasn't relevant to the topic at hand.

In your last comments in one video, you said,

"I hope God is proud of the people on the front line who are willing to risk the lives of God's creation. People go out of the front lines to get to say this is not okay. God says wherever you are, whether you're in Boston, whether you're in New York, whether you're in Atlanta or Minneapolis, that God is watching over you, and that is my creation using the blessings I gave them to stand up for justice. All of us are required to do that in some way."

This was a very heartfelt prayer, and may Allah answer your prayers. But please include other innocent souls who have been victims of oppression, racism, and torture, which I have listed above. I will maintain that no other oppression or injustice on earth compares to the merciless killing of unborn babies. Approximately 2 billion unborn humans have been killed worldwide since 1973, which is 2 billion souls who left the earth with silent screams. They have been erased from our hearts, our minds, and our lips, and we stay quiet about the greatest crime against humanity.

You and I believe in the Quranic verse, which alludes to Judgement Day, and we will be asked by our Creator about the children who were killed, *'for what crime was she killed?'* (Quran, 81:9). Let's hope we don't have to answer that and start the work of correcting this injustice While we are on this earth.

20.1 How Should You and Socialists Respond?

In-kind. I hope you have seen that it is possible to engage in constructive debate. You and your supporters may get a pleasant surprise when reading my letter because it is not what you expected. Your polarised discourses with those whom you disagree with usually end up in a dangerous place. This letter has been polite yet challenging, and I make no apologies for calling you out on your opinions, which are bathed in miscalculation, divisiveness, and manufactured rage. I don't use this new thing called sarcasm; these are for people who do not have arguments to offer. I expect you and your comrades to do the same, i.e., a point by point rebuttal of my opinions. We won't have to agree on everything.

This open letter offers you the red pill that I hope will lead to a significant change in thinking, which I mentioned earlier. Both you and I come from Arab and Asian backgrounds, respectively, and are masters of understanding crowd psychology and manipulating the 'madness of crowds' to our advantage. I stole this phrase from Douglas Murray, who wrote a book with the same title. I am not referring to peaceful protestors when I state the 'madness of crowds.' The advantage of a letter correspondence is that we are not playing to a crowd. There are no emotions to harness and redirect. It is just brute arguments laid out like bare bones. And I hope that both the left and the right can engage in a long-overdue dialogue and polite debate. I look forward to your response, Sister. You may think letter correspondences may take too long and divert your attention away from your activism. Make a video response instead. Other readers should send detailed responses to the arguments presented. I have started to read your book, '*We Are Not Here to Be Bystanders,*' and if we engage in dialogue, I will be sure there will be a few things I will pick out and discuss in due course, *inshallah*. I also hope that some points I raised above are answered in your book.

20.2 A Message to Conservative Readers

As this is an open letter, I hope this reaches out to your supporters on the left and the Conservatives/Republicans. So, my message to fellow Conservatives across the pond is this. Before Floyd's murder, when COVID spread was in full swing, it had affected BAME communities the most because of biological reasons. However, another catalyst is the lower socio-economic conditions they live in and in highly dense populations. This got me thinking. The higher infection rates and death rates amongst BAME need to be resolved.

The vaccine research that is going on is underway and will take care of the biological aspect, but the socio-economic conditions require urgent review. As Conservatives, we know the answer is to propel communities to better wealth, education, and opportunities. That is why we must shout loud (not in mass protests… COVID-19, remember?) about real solutions. We must be more resolute, more fervent in wanting this to happen, to propel people from poverty to prosperity. We are too 'conservative' for our attitude, so we need to generate that passion that we see in our fellow Socialist activists, not through sloganeering but shouting through the airwaves with concrete plans that will see this happen and to engage in lively and productive debate with those who have differing views. I will borrow the motto from our Socialist friends, *'**Workers of the world, unite and fight!'** and change it for us, and it goes like this, *'**Capitalists of the world, unite and solve!'***.

As far as Republicans are concerned, I think they have lost their bearings, and the negative publicity about Trump is not helping. When President George W. Bush, Mitt Romney, and Colin Powell say that they may vote for Joe Biden, there is a severe problem that the GOP faces that need addressing fast.

This is the time to go back to your roots and your foundation. Democrats can NEVER go back to their foundation because it is based initially on slavery, lynching, Ku Klux Klan, segregation, and so on. Yet, today's democrats denounce David Duke, from Louisiana, one of the most recognizable figures of the American radical right, a neo-Nazi, long time Klan leader as the Grand Wizard of the Knights of the Ku Klux Klan, and currently an international speaker. However, you can go back to your foundation with pride because the GOP was created to abolish slavery, and the great Republican hero, Abraham Lincoln, was murdered because of it.

The Republican party was the first party to have a first Hispanic governor; it passed the 14th Amendment, the 15th Amendment, and the 19th Amendment. It established Howard University to advance education among Black folks. It opposed Plessy Vs. Ferguson, it produced the first African-American senator, it outlawed the KKK, it passed the 1875 Civil rights Act, it selected a former slave to be chair its National Convention in 1884, it produced the first women mayors, it created the first Jewish Cabinet Secretary, it passed the Indian Citizenship Act, it produced the first Hispanic senator, it produced the first Asian-American senator, it called to end segregation in the military, it integrated the University of Mississippi, and it brought the 1957 Civil Rights Act.

I don't mind calling out fellow Conservatives who I think are wrong. I don't have feathers to ruffle nor an image to maintain. I had noticed when I observed conversations between White folks are more on the right (possibly Alt-right supporters or Tea Party? Not sure) and Black folks, there has been a sense of being judgemental on the Black folks. I sense an air of superiority by these small numbers of

White folks. They would hide behind '*oh its political correctness gone mad*' and not seek to understand what BAME communities are facing. They may think that institutional racism is a myth. As mentioned before, twice, when Black Lives Matter's slogan is used, many Conservatives would dismiss this as a request for specialist treatment. They would quickly divert to using the slogan '*All Lives Matter*' to ignore what BLM wants to accomplish. If they felt that all lives mattered, they would have made more effort to ensure that all communities got equal opportunity instead of waiting for BLM to come through and then react to it with the alternative slogan. EVERYONE should be allies of *Black Lives Matter*. Perish the thought that it would ruin your Conservative credentials. It won't.

Abraham Lincoln and the Republican Party knew Black lives mattered, and they did something about it to the howling opposition of those who wanted to keep slavery, segregation, and lynching. The Republicans need to re-connect with the Black communities, the very reason the GOP was created. **YOUR EXISTENCE AS A PARTY IS BASED ON THE FIGHT FOR THE RIGHTS OF BLACK LIVES**. The GOP must be an ally of BLM. I hope they are. BLM is one of many injustices around the world that I have alluded to throughout this letter. If we can get it right with BLM and institutional racism, then we can address other injustices in parallel. There are a good few Black and BAME folks who are Conservative.

I would encourage fellow White Conservatives to have courageous conversations with them. Don't assume that our life experiences will be the same because we all have the same political affiliation. They won't be. Here in the UK, there is an issue with Islamophobia within Conservative ranks, and it is down to us (Muslims) to educate and have courageous conversations within our own Party. A case in point, and I know that 100% of White folks would not have experienced this 'new normal' (unless you are a White Muslim woman) that we as a Muslim family experienced recently. There had been incidents of acid attacks two years ago in London, against Muslim women wearing headscarves. It targeted them for acid attacks on their faces. My wife wears the headscarf, and she once told me she had been fearful of someone in our local area, which looked like he was carrying a bottle of acid. When I heard this, I bought packs of water bottles to put them in her car, and I have always strategically positioned these bottles inside her car so they could be within easy reach if needed. I also trained my daughter (seven at the time) on what to do if her mother was distraught and shocked after an acid attack. This has become the new norm for us, that I would always replenish her car with bottles of water strategically positioned. It is good to have more sharing of experiences such as this.

I have noticed that there is skepticism of Diversity & Inclusion (D&I) programs as we go further and further right and maybe venturing into the spheres of 'Alt-right' or White rights activism. There seems to be a narrative amongst these groups that White culture is under threat and that D&I is meant to crowd out White folks. I deal with White supremacy and non-violent White rights arguments in an extended video response (details below). D&I is an enabler inclusive of everyone regardless of race or gender. They should roll these programs out in all companies, and it is a chance for us to learn from each other. BAME communities could even learn from the experiences of White folks. It's a 2-way street. Embrace it.

While much of the Conservative media (Breitbart, Fox News, Daily Wire) is focused on condemning the violence, thinking there is a conspiracy to oust President Trump and acknowledging that the agitators are destroying the message of peaceful protesters, you (i.e. the Conservative reader) should listen to the statements of the peaceful protestors. What is their message? That institutional racism exists, and there have to be structural changes to eliminate it. Although a small number, there is police brutality, they cause the most significant problems to the police force and racial profiling in the US and the UK. There should be more education and reform of the police. Break out of your cocoon of listening to Conservative media only and avail yourself of other materials so we can have a broader understanding and appreciation of different life experiences. Have you come across Prof. Carol Anderson of Emory University, and her talk on *White rage – the Unspoken Truth About Our Racial Divide?'* If not, why not? Or what about James A. White Sr.? His speech on *50 years of racism* is an eye-opener. What is it about Black life experiences of injustices you are afraid to listen to?

Finally, PLEASE end the polarisation of conversation. Reach out to folks on the left or others who do not agree with you so we can come to mutual understanding or just agree to disagree. People on the left are not viruses, so please don't treat them like they are. They want to change the world for a better place, just like we do, but we have different mechanisms to achieve this. Allow yourself to understand others and allow yourself to change your mind. One of the best speeches on unity I heard in recent times was from a Democrat. You will recall the 2000 elections and the run for the presidency between George W. Bush and Al Gore. It pleased me when Bush became President, but I appreciated the message of unity that Al Gore delivered in his concession speech after weeks of wrangling and controversy. His message still rings true today. Or in 2008, when John McCain lost to Barack Obama. McCain was magnanimous in his concession speech and was proud of the fact that Obama was elected as President because of what it meant for the African-American community. I, too, was proud that he was elected and what it represented for the Black communities, even though I was on the other side of the fence. Listen to those two speeches again.

Go back to your foundation with pride and rise from the ashes so you can take a march forward once again and close the economic gaps between communities and bring prosperity to all of them. That is what Conservatives do best.

20.3 A Prayer

Back to you, Sister Linda. A belated lockdown Eid Mubarak. May God bless you and your family. May God strengthen George Floyd's family and ease their pain. May He have mercy on other souls who have been taken away. They are all too many to name, but God knows who they are. May God also understand the whole of Mankind during this time of a global pandemic, social unrest, injustices, fear, and uncertainty. May He guide us towards hope, peace, and unity for our children's sake. Amen/Ameen.

CHAPTER 21

FINAL THOUGHT AND SONG

When I was at boarding school in the late 80s, we used to have morning assemblies where pupils would say or do whatever they did and end with music or song to ponder over the message. So, let me end with the link to a song that encapsulates this letter in a nutshell and embodies the directives that the prominent leaders of the 20th Century espoused; Martin Luther King Jr, Mahatma Gandhi, Nelson Mandela, the Dalai Lama. Apart from Dalai Lama and the Pope, we have no such leaders today and too many wannabe leaders. Let us ponder over this song, which is entitled, *'Where's the Love*?'

https://www.youtube.com/watch?v=YsRMoWYGLNA

Video Links

My brief speech to the Conservative Party Conference in 2001 on Islam and Terrorism (**3 mins 35s**).

https://www.youtube.com/watch?v=CZ0NuDBqX_A&list=PLsJmP_PfDlSSiYqLoy5kg38v5Bn3VEqEh&index=2&t

My brief speech to the Conservative Party Conference in 2006 on Islam, terrorism and Community Cohesion (**2 mins 45s**)

https://www.youtube.com/watch?v=Z0wzaHowteM&list=PLsJmP_PfDlSSiYqLoy5kg38v5Bn3VEqEh&index=2

My video response to the far right, White supremacy, and the New Zealand terrorist attacked a mosque in March 2019 (**3 hrs 30 mins**).

https://youtu.be/2a-piFzrceU

Miscellaneous - Responses to Other Socialist Activists in the US

1) Letter to Black Lives Matter from a Conservative Ally- No Condemnation of the Knee on Neck Toddler Incident

Dear BLM,

I am a Conservative ally of BLM, and I applaud the excellent work you have done to raise consciousness about racism through peaceful protests and encourage courageous conversations. I am concerned that the goodwill that you have from across the board and around the world has and is being tarnished by thugs who are using BLM to attack businesses, burn buildings, attack police officers, and also a minority of the thugs who are using the new police-free zones to commit crimes. I know they do not represent your peaceful movement. And I believe that you have been trying to respond to these activities that try to harm BLM. I read your op-ed (on a website) where you articulate the campaign of disinformation and conspiracies against your movement. I agree with the following comments you made:

"Domestic and international disinformation agents work to appear bigger and more relevant than they are. They misappropriate images of Black people and impersonate organizers and movement leaders in an attempt to cause chaos and harm to our communities. History shows us that organized disinformation threatens the public discourse and is a tried-and-true way to undermine the liberation work of champions for racial justice."

What has been very disturbing is one such thug and child abuser, Isaiah Jackson, misused the name of BLM to replicate the knee-on-neck (and knee-on-back as per Tony Timpa in 2016) on the two-year-old toddler? Why hasn't there been a fierce condemnation of this incident? Agreed, there are multiple injustices taking place, and one cannot campaign against all at the same time. But this incident used your right name to make a political point by abusing a White toddler. You agree that other incidents of knee-on-neck brutality by police, post-Floyd, have been widely reported in the US and UK because the knee-on-neck is symbolic of Floyd's struggle and eventual woeful murder. I expected the media to report these subsequent incidents, and they have.

The toddler incident is also connected to Floyd, but most media outlets have not addressed this, neither has BLM stated to condemn this heinous abuse. What is it about this toddler incident that doesn't merit public condemnation or publicity, but the other knee-on-neck experiences post-Floyd, do? I am at a loss to explain the difference. Perhaps Jackson has been arrested, and that other killer of Breonna Taylor is on the loose (someone with whom I had a dialogue with made this point); hence Taylor's and Floyd's cases would receive publicity. But with Floyd, Chauvin was charged, and subsequent incidents of knee-on-neck brutalities by police were widely publicized even though the police officers in question were arrested. So that argument would not hold. What is it about the toddler incident that does not merit mass publicity and condemnation by friends who had been vocal about Floyd's death and other injustices over the last few months?

Many thanks.
Peace and power to you.
Your friend and ally

Short Dialogue with Socialists on the Knee on Neck Toddler Incident

My Comments on the Toddler Incident

Hi, any thoughts on the simulation of the knee-on-neck action by Isaiah Jackson on a two-year-old toddler who was in distress? Also, the knee on the toddler's back by another person. The caption in the photo was BLM MF. This guy is misusing the image of BLM…and to use a two-year-old to do this is beyond humanity. Should there not be protests about this? Correct, the toddler did not die, but it was woefully abused by combining the pressure's actions on the back (Tony Timpa 2016) and pressure on the neck (George Floyd 2020).

I have seen no rage nor condemnation of this incident nor protests by groups who have protested against George

Floyd's murder by a similar method. I cannot understand the silence here.

Reply from 'Caleb'

I have a simple explanation for you. They already arrested him, but they still haven't arrested Breonna Taylor's killers. Edit: they detained just one of George Floyd's killers for tax evasion, but not for killing George Floyd over $20.

Reply from 'Rob'

Protest is for when the perpetrator is not held accountable. Thanks.

My Reply

Thanks, Caleb and Rob. Good points and it made me think. But from what I understand, Derek Chauvin and other related officers were arrested and charged. But the protests continued and spread to other countries on behalf of Floyd. If this is wrong, then I stand corrected. Even if people do not protest on behalf of the toddler, there should be a loud condemnation of the act, which abuses BLM by abusing a toddler? The silence is still puzzling.

Reply from 'Aaron'

It's not just about George Floyd. He was just the final spark that lit all the matches. There isn't a systemic issue of Blacks kneeling on toddlers' necks. This is a one-off incident all condemn that the country.

Reply from 'Caleb'

It is essential to keep in mind that BLM is only a collection of various community organizers and the communities that subscribe to them being supported by loose bands of noncommittal supporters. They are not training anyone to kneel on the necks of toddlers. They aren't organized state police.

My Reply

Thanks again for your reply. It is much appreciated. I understand the point made by Aaron that Floyd is the spark that lit the matches. I also take the fact that Blacks leaning on toddler's necks is not systemic. The toddler in question who suffered wouldn't see it that way. What is the definition of '*systemic*' in police officers kneeling on necks? I agree that this is a one-off incident and that the whole country would condemn it, but the problem is I have not seen that level of condemnation when I look at the mainstream media. Why shouldn't this specific incident be worthy of outright condemnation in the most resolute terms (if not through protests)?

Because Isaiah Jackson used two things here. First, the BLM name was misused, and as Caleb said, BLM doesn't train people to kneel on the necks of toddlers. All the more reason, there should have been a massive uproar from BLM and other allies for the woeful misuse of its name, which seeks justice for all. Second, the kneeling on the toddler's neck tactic is an insult to George Floyd (who was described as peaceful and a gentle giant by his brother, Terrence), and using his death to make a political point by making a toddler suffer is rancid at the least.

Because this particular tactic used by Chauvin killed Floyd (and another tactic on pressing on the back used against Tony Timpa), that lit the match then Isaiah Jackson's stunt, which used the same tactics, and linked them with BLM, should have caused an outcry among the very people who took to the streets. But as I said, there is relative silence from these groups. And they would seem to condemn this incident only reactively rather than proactively. The toddler's White privilege did not help, and it suffered.

Another reason for the need for a proactive public condemnation by BLM and its allies is many police officers who joined the BLM protesters and took the knee to support racial justice. These officers condemned Chauvin, and they denounce the minority of officers who are racist and kill innocent civilians. Chauvin et al. do not represent most police officers, which is a point well made by officers who took the knee.

Likewise, Muslims would publicly condemn the actions of a minority of Muslims who engage in terrorism. So, it is only right that BLM and its allies make a public statement to condemn Jackson's actions fiercely. I am getting that the toddler's life doesn't matter enough to be a proactive mass condemnation.

Caleb made an excellent point in the first comment that Jackson was arrested, but Breonna's killers were not. This is true. And all of us would support Jackson being detained by the police, and we expect the police to find and arrest Breonna's killers. Hence this is an indirect argument not to defund the police but to reform. As has been gleaned from Caleb's comment, we expect the police to do their jobs, so defunding them and abolishing the police force (one activist, Linda Sarsour, said they should arrest ALL police officers) will make it more difficult to arrest criminals. Many Thanks, as always, I appreciate your thoughts.

Reply from 'Carla'

Maybe the issue is as simple as the fact that there is so much crap going on simultaneously that you can't possibly keep up! For one, I do not understand who Isiah Jackson is or what you are talking about, and it's not like I ignore the news. When people become overwhelmed by events, they tend to narrow their focus to concentrate on the stuff right in front of their faces. I live in Seattle, and Trump sent his mercenaries our way to stir up trouble, so you bet my focus has shifted to what's going on in my backyard. That by NO MEANS implies that I don't care about what is going on in Portland or the incident you are alluding to.

Also, I think it is pretty disingenuous to accuse BLM of implying that this "toddler's life doesn't matter enough" because no official statement has been released addressing it. That does not make them hypocrites; everything in life is not an "either/or" situation! You are doing the equivalent of chastising someone for participating in a walk-a-thon to raise money for brain cancer as proof they don't give a sh*t about breast cancer, ALS, or the blind!

My Reply

Many thanks, Carla, for taking the time to reply and help me make sense of something that appears very peculiar to me. That you do not understand who Isaiah Jackson is even though you pay attention to the news is precisely the point I am making. Why isn't this being reported by the main news outlets?

I completely understand your point about a myriad of problems and challenges people face simultaneously; hence, people would narrow their focus on issues that they are directly affected by. And you emphasize the point that the focus on one issue does not negate concern for other issues. And a good analogy you drew is that if one campaign for a brain cancer charity doesn't mean you don't give a damn about different cancers. I agree with this analogy. This is why I have criticized BLM critics who charge the organization with being one-sided and ignore other injustices. BLM is not isolationist. They care about most injustices in the world regardless of color or creed, but addressing racism against Blacks is a starting point. That is why everyone should be allies of BLM.

I returned to the toddler's point and the relative silence from organizations and protesters, including BLM. You stated that my criticism of BLM's silence because the toddler's life did not matter enough, was disingenuous because BLM did not release an official statement. Again, this is precisely my point. Why didn't they come out with a message? Isaiah Jackson misused their good name when he performed the knee-on-the-neck action on the crying toddler, coupled with pressure on its back.

They did the same thing to Tony Timpa, who died later from the injury in 2016. The toddler received a double dose of brutality in one go in the name of '***BLM NOW MF***.' That is why I reiterate the point I made previously that BLM should have come out in loud condemnation of this child abuse in the same way many police officers condemned Chauvin's actions and joined the protesters or took the knee. And in the same way, Muslim communities would condemn a minority's actions that inflict terrorism in the name of Islam.

Caleb made an interesting point in his first response, where he implied that Isaiah was arrested; hence protests and public condemnation were not warranted. If protesters pick injustice, that's fine, and one cannot expect to protest about every single injustice around the world. But we can expect at least a public condemnation. People may ask why I am so fixated about the knee-on-the-neck and knee-on-the-back actions against the frightened toddler? Aaron showed that the Floyd incident was the last spark that lit the matches, which triggered multiple protests. Again, it is precisely because of this inciting incident against Floyd that further police acts on knee-on-the-neck of suspects were reported by the media widely, which led to some of these officers' arrests in the US and UK and worldwide condemnation. Floyd's murder is the trigger for the protests and media highlights of other knee-on-the neck brutality by police post-Floyd's death. That is why the New York Times even reported a police officer's knee-on-the-neck incident on a suspect in the UK.

Because these knee-on-neck actions by police are so symbolic of Floyd's situation, they merit reporting by the media even though the incidents are across the pond. They are all connected to Floyd's knee-on-neck brutality, which is the trigger point. That is why you would have heard of these incidents post-Floyd even though you may be facing Trump's henchmen or something else closer to home.

Now one could argue that the knee-on-neck (and knee-on-back) abuse against the frightened toddler is far worse than the reported incidents of police doing the same thing on suspects post-Floyd's death. Why far worse? Because an innocent child is being abused, the BLM name has been misused, and the criminal is also misusing Floyd's death for his twisted philosophy. *CNN, the BBC, CBNC, Al Jazeera, New York Times* made no mention of this incident as far as I am aware, but Fox News, *New York Post*, and the

Washington Post did. The latter set of media outlets may be regarded as being more on the political right. But this should not be about left or right. It is about right and wrong. When I looked at the Facebook posts of campaigners, commentators, and organizations (who were vocal during the protests) during the last few days after the toddler incident, there is no mention of this heinous act of child abuse. One commentator is enjoying herself in Ibiza, another commentator talked about the mental fitness of Kayne West, who registered to run for President under the Birthday Party, another commentator celebrated the release of Dennis Perry after 20 years of wrongful incarceration, yet another well-known activist in the US dared to put up a poster from the New York police department about a missing Muslim woman… after campaigning to defund the police and arrest ALL officers. It boggles the mind, doesn't it?

Thanks again for all of your responses. I take them seriously. We are on different parts of the political spectrum; so, we may not be comrades, but I see us as friends, and I value the courageous conversations we are having. However, I welcome further thoughts.

Should the Democrats Apologise to Brett Kavanaugh? Dialogue with a Socialist

The answer to the question is not. They had the right to question Kavanaugh about his alleged sexual harassment of Christine Ford. Democrats may call out and challenge Joe Biden with the same passion and enthusiasm they displayed two years ago. Below is a brief dialogue I had with a Socialist in the US about this glaring contradiction.

Dear Friend,

I hope you are well. I appreciate the short dialogue we had a few weeks ago concerning Isaiah Jackson's knee-on-neck abuse against a 2-year-old toddler. I welcome the various contributions that have been made. It is good to engage in dialogue, especially when there is an atmosphere of intolerance and hate. And I hope we have witnessed that it is possible to have decent, de-polarised conversations and given that I am a British Conservative (I stood for Parliament in 2005 against a sitting Labour-Socialist MP... one of the very few MPs I respect because of his commitment to the very foundation of the Labour Party which is Socialism, as opposed to the rest of Labour which seeks to dump its Socialist origins) that is why it has been possible to keep things civil. I am open-minded, which is why it has been easy to engage in discussions with people who hold different philosophies only two years ago, I spoke with the Russian Ambassador to Bangladesh (my country of origin) who explained why he thought that Russians were better under Communism than under the current free-market economy. I listened with interest.

I hope to engage with you again and attempt to understand an issue that I had raised on my Facebook post two years ago and is more relevant than ever after Kamala Harris was chosen as the Democrat VP candidate a few days ago. Your opinions would be highly appreciated.

I am not concerned about Harris's racial origins; I think Republican compatriots have gone bonkers *with their focus on this. ALL Americans other than the Native Americans have roots outside the US. Hence this whole racial debate is moot. I don't go for character assassinations; it is very un-British but what is important to me is integrity, transparency, and honesty. I had an issue with the Democrats' behavior during the Brett Kavanaugh hearings in 2018 in the way they seemed to have used Christine Ford's situation for their benefit to prevent Kavanaugh from assuming his position on the Supreme Court. Kamala Harris, Amy Klobuchar, Cory Booker, and Elizabeth Warren were quite vehement in their denunciation of Kavanaugh's alleged attempted rape of Ford. I watched the proceedings with great interest, **and at one-point, Kamala Harris** seemed to put Kavanaugh in a tight spot with her precision questioning. During Ford's hearing, Kamala told her that she believed her. You may also recall when the Socialist (pro-Sanders) activist, Linda Sarsour, burst into Kavanaugh's hearing as part of the Women's March to protest against him, and later she said that this was about justice. In January 2019, she said, "Watching rape culture play out on a national stage has retraumatized women and survivors nationwide," she said in the email. "But in response, we've turned our pain into power."*

After the proceedings ended, I drew some conclusions and made a prediction:

a) The Democrat senators who questioned Kavanaugh received a lot of limelight, understandably. They would use this opportunity to advance their careers. It turns out that most of them did when Booker, Warren, Harris, and Klobuchar put their hats in the ring to bid for the presidential nomination. Klobuchar was fascinating. She said that the Kavanaugh hearings and injustices against women because of sexual harassment motivated her to throw her hat into the ring.

b) I predicted that the Democrats would let down Christine Ford when the hearings were over. They seemed to use her plight for politics. It proved me correct when she appeared to be ditched after they confirmed Kavanaugh. While the Democrat mentioned above senators advanced their careers, Ford was and continues to be in hiding with no hope of leading an everyday life. I am sure that Nancy Pelosi said there might be a follow-up, but there hasn't been. A few weeks ago, when I checked the Facebook pages and the websites of these senators who competed in the primaries, and Nancy Pelosi's, there was no mention of Christine Ford anywhere. This appalled me. No one talks about Ford now. I am now beginning to understand what Brett Kavanaugh and the Republican Senator Chuck Grassley (who chaired the hearings) meant that the Democrats were being very political and wanted to take down Kavanaugh because of his pro-life stance. At the time, I thought these were excuses to divert attention away from Kavanaugh's alleged sexual harassment of Ford. But in the aftermath of what has happened and the capitalization of the Democrat senators' fame which led them to seek higher office, and a complete detachment from Ford, who has received no further support.

I can empathize with what Kavanaugh and Grassley said. Since then, I seemed to have ventured into the Twilight Zone, where I look at what these Democrat senators and Linda Sarsour in the light of allegations of Joe Biden's digital penetration (I'll call it digital rape) of Tara Reade. Other than the Conservatives' expected highlight of this case, the Democrats have been collectively silent on this matter or seemed to have excused Biden. The major media outlets seem to be quiet now after a brief stint on this story. This is a major 'WHAT THE F***?' moment for me, as there seems to be a mass cognitive dissonance or CONSCIOUS BIAS here.

At this point, I have to give credit to your (left-wing group) for calling out Biden on this. I read two posts where you reminded members that Biden is an alleged sexual harasser and no different from Trump. This is the only honest appraisal of Biden I have seen from the left in the US that has come from your group. The rest of the Democrats are silent or have taken contradictory approaches when challenged. An even more critical story I saw unfold in the Twilight Zone is the veteran feminist campaigner, Angela Davis, who announced her support for Biden so the left could more easily influence him. I also see Rabia Chaudry, who is an attorney and a vociferous campaigner for the release of Adnan Sayed, who is in jail for the murder of Hae Min Lee in 1999. She believes Adnan is innocent, hence wants him released. She was quite vocal in the "Twittosphere" against Brett Kavanaugh only to support Joe Biden in the upcoming elections. The following are the summaries of these are the contradictory approaches I have noticed:

1. **Kamala Harris on Kavanaugh**: "I sat through those hearings. Brett Kavanaugh lied to the U.S. Senate and, most importantly, to the American people. He was put on the Court through a sham process, and his place on the Court is an insult to the pursuit of truth and justice. He must be impeached." (Twitter, 15th Sept. 2019). She also told Christine Ford, "I believe you."

Kamala Harris on Biden: "I believe them, and I respect them being able to tell their story and having the courage to do it," Harris said at a presidential campaign event in Nevada. When asked if Biden should run for president, Harris said,

"He's going to have to make that decision for himself. I wouldn't tell him what to do." (*Daily Caller*, April 2019)

2. **Amy Klobuchar on Kavanaugh**: "Let us never forget what courage looks like" (showing a picture of Christine Ford taking her oath. Facebook post, 15th Sept 2019)

Amy Klobuchar on Biden: "We need a President who cares about others, instead of himself. We need a President who believes service is about sacrifice, not self-interest. We need Joe Biden in the White House." (Facebook page 24th May 2020)

3. **Elizabeth Warren on Kavanaugh**: "The fight against Kavanaugh. You don't want to wake up the day after Brett Kavanaugh gets confirmed as the next Supreme Court Justice of the United States and say: I could've done more to help stop it. Now is the time to make calls, write letters, and do whatever you can to speak out against Kavanaugh's confirmation to the Supreme Court. This fight is in the hands of the people." (Facebook post, 18th September 2018)

She also said, "Let's be clear: Brett Kavanaugh is NOT entitled to a seat on the Supreme Court. We're going to keep fighting his nomination with everything we've got & made our voices heard." (Facebook post, 29th September 2019)

Elizabeth Warren on Biden: "This is the right way to conduct oversight. Thank you, Joe Biden, for committing to appointing a genuinely independent Inspector General and tackling corruption head-on." (Facebook post, 12th May 2020)

4. **Cory Booker on Kavanaugh**: "I'm here to call on folk to understand that in a moral moment there is no neutral. In a moral moment there are no bystanders," Booker told the

crowd. "You are either complicit in the evil, you are either contributing to the wrong, or you are fighting against it." Booker also said, "It doesn't say that I sit in the valley of the shadow of death. It doesn't say I'm sitting on the side-lines in the valley of the shadow of death. It says I am walking through the valley of the shadow of death. It says I am taking agency that I am going to make it through this crisis," Booker said. "And so, I am calling on everyone right now who understands what's at stake, who understands who Kavanaugh is. My ancestors said, 'if someone shows you who they are, believe them the first time.' He has shown us who he is." (*National Review* 24th July 2018)

Cory Booker on Biden: Sen. Cory Booker says sexual assault allegation against Biden, which he has denied, should be investigated: "Investigate the claims, and I celebrate Joe Biden for standing up and saying the same thing." "I stand with Joe on his nomination," he adds. (*The View*, Twitter, 8th May 2020)

5. **Nancy Pelosi on Kavanaugh**: "Today is a profoundly heart-breaking day for women, girls, and families across America." "Courageous women risked their safety and well-being to speak the truth about this nomination. Tens of thousands more joined them to share their own harrowing sexual assault stories, at significant personal risk. Yet, Senate Republicans chose to send a clear message to all women: do not speak out, and if you do -- do not expect to be heard, believed, or respected. (6th October 2018, Speaker.gov website, after Brett Kavanaugh's confirmation).

Nancy Pelosi on Biden: "I have complete respect for the MeToo movement. I have four daughters and one son. And there's a lot of excitement around the idea that women will be heard and be listened to." "I have a great comfort level with the situation as I see it, with all the respect in the world for any woman who comes forward, with all the highest regard for Joe Biden, and that's what I have to say about that." (*The Independent*, 30th April 2020)

6. **Linda Sarsour on Kavanaugh:** "I will be able to tell my daughters and future grandchildren that I STOOD UP. I was not and will not be silent when our bodies and rights are on the line. #CancelKavanaugh." (Sarsour's Twitter quoting *ABC* News Twitter feed, 4th September 2018, after she stormed into Kavanaugh's hearing as part of the Women's March)

Linda Sarsour on Biden: "It's no secret that I have disagreements with both VP Joe Biden & Senator Kamala Harris. But I know what I need to do -- Elect the Biden-Harris ticket and prepare to hold them accountable in the White House. Remember, sometimes the hardest thing to do is the right thing to do. Let's DEFEAT FASCISM. (Sarsour's Facebook post, 12th August 2020)

7. **Rabia Chaudry on Kavanaugh**: "The presumption of innocence applies in court. This is a damn job interview." (Twitter, 24th Sep. 2018)

"What kind of a shit judge would dismiss a sworn statement by a WOMAN WHO WAS GANG RAPED" (In response to Kavanaugh's angry answer to Diane Feinstein's question on Julie Swetnick, Twitter 27th Sept. 2018)

"Kavanaugh wasn't raging because he is innocent. He was raging because one woman dared to try and hold him accountable." (Twitter, 28th Sept. 2018)

"Yes, it was planned 36 years ago when Kavanaugh attempted to rape Ford and covered it up ever since." (In response to the GOP tweet stating that what was done to Kavanaugh was planned and politics at its worst. Twitter, 29th Sept. 2018).

Rabia Chaudry on Biden: Rabia posted an event, 'Pakistani Americans for Biden — A Community Fired up for Change!'

Disturbing Questions

What exactly is going on here? I am sure we can agree that digital rape (Biden) is far more severe than attempted rape (Kavanaugh). Yet Biden has been given the benefit of the doubt quite liberally. I cannot understand this contradiction. What is going through the minds of many Democrats who can clearly see their contradictory approaches to sexual harassment, and yet sleep very well at night? I would expect some people on the left to call out Biden. Other than your organization [***deleted***], there is collective silence on the matter on the left. Their relative silence is an assault on women victims of sexual harassment, and I believe they are urinating on the "MeToo" movement now after showing support initially during the Kavanaugh hearings. In her recent Facebook post supporting Biden, Linda Sarsour's meek demeanor indeed occupies the stratosphere of the Twilight Zone. What if the veteran feminist campaigner, Angela Davis's open support of Biden? Some women's lives matter, and others don't.

I would be grateful if you would help me understand what is going on here? I am seeking a genuine dialogue (I am not a Trump supporter, by the way). I will end with the following question, 'should Kamala Harris apologize to Brett Kavanaugh?'

Response from the Socialist Friend

Honestly, it's better not to post that. We (women) are VERY aware of both her and the DNC's wilful ignorance about Biden's allegations. We don't need a reminder of the other women who have completely "forgotten" about the accusations to support him.

My Reply

Thanks for that. Ok, I will respect your decision and won't post it. I just wanted to understand why the other women senators and campaigners had forgotten about Biden's allegations when they were so vocal about Kavanaugh. Sexual harassment should be above politics and a unifying factor about injustices against women, as exemplified by the "MeToo" movement, and this should be the major news in the media. But what I see now (no thanks to the Republicans) is an irrelevant focus on Kamala's racial background. Why are the women Democrat Senators and campaigners (Linda Sarsour, Angela Davis) supporting Biden? If it is to stop Trump, it still makes little sense because sexual harassment against women victims is a more critical issue than Trump's personality? I have found the [***deleted***] to be the only left group in the US so far which has shown integrity and consistency by calling out Biden for alleged sexual harassment, which is why I wanted to get your perspective of this contradiction and why there is a veil of silence.

I forgot to mention in the main post [***Note to the reader, I added this story in the main post later after this dialogue ended***] about Rabia Chaudry, a famous attorney who tweeted in 2018 that Kavanaugh had planned to rape Ford and that Julie Swetnick was gang-raped (which included Kavanaugh). Only recently, she posts an event, 'Pakistani Americans for Biden -- A Community Fired Up For Change.' One could not make this up. Even though my post is not public, it would be great to get your insight into what exactly is going on here and why firm advocates of women's rights are now supporting Biden. Your thoughts on my original post would be welcome. Thanks.

Response from Socialist Friend

Honestly, I couldn't tell you why these people who have built their entire lives fighting the oppression and abuse of women would completely dump their entire value systems to support this person. My psychology background would tell me it's from pure fear of what Trump can do, but if they researched what is happening, they would know that men like Joe Biden are the cause, Trump is the symptom. There's a good chance that the formation of an authoritarian regime has been in the cards for several years, if not decades. Trump just seems to be more upfront about it.

My Reply

Thanks [***deleted***] for taking the time to provide a useful insight… great that your psychology background has come in handy! We might be on opposite parts of the political spectrum, but I do respect Bernie Sanders. He does seem to be a man of integrity and honesty. A similar personality to the veteran Socialist Labour MP, Dennis Skinner, whom I stood against in the Parliamentary elections in 2005. Honest and transparent guy. (End of dialogue)

Thoughts on the Above Mini Discussion

The US's Socialist acquaintance was very honest about her views of the Democrats' silence on Joe Biden's alleged sexual harassment. She said that people were more concerned about what Trump could do and that Trump was a symptom, not a cause. I did not pursue this discussion as she felt uncomfortable about being let down by the Democrats and didn't want to remind her of this, so I ended here. But the question that comes to mind after her response is, 'what could be more concerning than the abuse of human rights, in this case, sexual harassment of women?' The reason for asking this question is that Trump had been rightly criticized for the secret recording of a meeting in 2005, where he fantasized about kissing Arianne Zucker and touching her private parts without her consent. Any human being would condemn this. What struck me was that Trump fantasised in 2005 what Joe Biden allegedly acted out in 1993.

What is this concern about Trump that Democrats are willing to observe collective silence on sexual harassment against women after being so vociferous two years ago? What issue is more important than human rights in the context of sexual harassment against women? Racism may come to mind, which is on par with harassment against women. And Democrats may think Trump's apparent racism may be more critical than Biden's digital rape of a woman. Again, this does not help the Democrats because Kamala Harris implied that Biden was a racist during the Primaries when she accused him of supporting segregationist senators. Biden made an overtly racist remark when he told a radio host that you aren't Black if you have to choose between Trump and Biden. So, I ask again, what is it about Trump that Democrats feel they have to remain collectively silent on Biden's alleged sexual harassment and let down women victims and the "Me Too" movement?

The same question goes to Republicans and Conservatives who have fallen silent on this critical issue after initial publicity. Instead, they are traveling down an irrelevant route of questioning Kamala's race identity and Biden's cognitive decline.

4) Undercurrents of Anti-White Racism. Let's Stop This Hate Before It Becomes a Tsunami Response to an author who believes that ALL Whites are racist.

Greetings from the UK, Marley. Thanks for an informative article entitled, *'Yes My Dear, All White People Are Racists.'*

I would argue that to claim all White people are racist is a racist statement because it doesn't take into account the actions many White people have taken to combat racism. I don't recognize the phrase 'reverse racism.' There is no such thing. Racism is racism, period. It's not enough being non-racist; people have to be anti-racist. And there are plenty of White people who have demonstrated so. Actions are more important than words. So, when they act (and you gave a list of activities they had taken), these would all be dismissed by you because they must start from the point of admitting that they are racist in the first place.

If White people admit that historically there has been White oppression of Blacks in the US from slavery through to overt racism in the 1960s and that now we have come a long way and many Whites are anti-racist, why should they rewind and start by saying they are racist? What makes a racist, a racist? Superiority complex and hatred of the other because of their color or culture. And I have observed racism by Whites against non-Whites, Blacks against Whites (Nation of Islam cult group), Whites against Asians, Asians against Whites, Asians against Blacks, and so on. Racism is universal, an awkward and paradoxical reality.

White anti-racists who speak and act against racial injustices would be alienated when you tell them that they are still racist and that their anti-racist actions mean nothing unless they admit they are racist. You and I know that talk is cheap until it is backed by action. In the cases of White anti-racist campaigners you mentioned, the reverse seems to be accurate, that action is affordable and that it needs to be backed by talk.

Moreover, the talk or starting point needs to be an admission that they are racists. I guess this is the main issue of contention here. If you want anti-racist White folk to admit they are racists despite their opposite actions and despite their admission that many of their ancestors were racists and oppressive, then this implies two things:

1. **That these White folks are the same as current White supremacists** and racists who hate Blacks and people of color. The starting point of admission of racism, which you wish to see, applies to present White supremacists and racists, not White anti-racist commentators and activists. You have conflated the two groups. I have tried to engage with White supremacists and racists, and I know there is a difference between their philosophies and the philosophies and actions of White anti-racists. We can agree on this. Hence, you are alienating fellow White friends who are no longer like their ancestors or current White supremacists. Why should their starting point be 'I am a racist?'

2. **That Martin Luther King, Malcolm X, and other veteran campaigners failed** in their work towards racial justice and equality. We have come a long way since the racism of the 60s and 70s that some of us have observed and even further away from the era of slavery. MLK etc. did NOT

FAIL. They succeeded. And when I review the '**I Have a Dream**' speech, he was very inclusive and wanted to see White people and Black people joining hands together and doing things together. I do not know this language from anti-White privilege commentators and activists. Malcolm X (Malik Al-Shabazz) is often quoted when he was part of the Nation of Islam. He admitted that his anti-White views had changed when he went to Mecca during the Hajj and engaged with White Muslims. He had transformed after embracing Orthodox Islam and had a universal outlook. Let's not forget Mahatma Gandhi, who helped liberate India from British Colonial rule. He never advocated revenge against Whites; neither did he consider all of them to be racists. He just wanted equal rights for the Indians initially and then independence. I do not see a leader today like Martin Luther King or Malik Al-Shabazz or Mahatma Gandhi. **I lament that their elevated views about humanity and brotherhood are in suspended animation in the 20th Century. The 21st Century seems in reverse gear beyond retro and faster than the speed of light, as I see more discord between human beings than unity. Bridges are burning fast.**

Some Questions Come to Mind

1. Do you still maintain that White anti-racists must utter the words, 'I am a racist?' If so, why?

2. What is the difference between a White supremacist/racist and a White anti-racist if the starting point of origin for both groups is, 'I am a racist?'

3. Why do you dismiss the anti-racist languages, actions, and thoughts of White anti-racists because they haven't uttered the words, 'I am a racist?' Why is a statement that is no longer valid more critical current thoughts and actions? All critics of politicians argue that politicians say things but don't act on them. Your worldview is the reverse.

4. If the answers to the three questions above do not challenge you to review your position, then it implies that you consider White racism to be genetic. That Whites are born with this genetic disorder. Is this correct, or have I misread you?

5. I have mentored a White manager on what it is to be BAME and the experiences we've had. The conversation was two ways because I was also interested to know her perspective on being White and a woman. We had great discussions, and she told me that she tries to be inclusive and ensures there is diversity among her team and that everyone is respected. She condemns racism wherever she sees it. Please tell me why I should say to her to admit being a racist when she isn't?

6. In the world of multiculturalism, there will be interracial relations. I have heard racists within my Asian community, and the White community describe bi-racial people as mongrels or have no identity. Let's think of a bi-racial person who has a White father and a Black mother. Is that person partly racist, half a racist…what is he?

7. A few weeks ago, I wrote to Black Lives Matter USA about the horrific incident where Isaiah Jackson put his knee on a two-year-old toddler and had the caption, 'BLM Now MF' on his photo. This did not get the comprehensive media

coverage, which you would expect as it is symbolic of what happened to George Floyd. I explained to BLM that I am a Conservative ally of BLM and that all people should be allies. Some unfortunate rogue elements have infiltrated BLM to destroy businesses and livelihoods and burn buildings, affecting Black business owners and customers they serve... a 2020 version of Tulsa 1921 when White people went on a rampage to burn Black-owned businesses and destroy families. I asked BLM why they did not condemn this child abuse incident as it was done in their name, and I know that BLM would never advocate this, so it is right they come out and condemn this incident. I have not had a reply. I had a short dialogue with a Socialist organization in the US about this incident, and they did not give a convincing answer. So maybe you can help me here. Why has this incident not received the sweeping condemnation it deserves? You will agree that if a White man had done the same thing against a Black toddler, this would have been world news, and rightly so. But given the colors are reversed, there is stone silence when there should have been equal vociferousness. What is the explanation for this? This is a racist incident, as well as child abuse. There may be some underlying anti-White narrative that is slowly building in the anti-racist movement, explaining the silence on this matter. But I would like to understand your thoughts on this.

8. The great doyen of the Civil Rights movement, Martin Luther King Jr., said, *"The (Black man) needs the White man to free him from his fears. The White man needs the (Black man) to free him from his guilt. A doctrine of Black supremacy is as evil as a doctrine of White supremacy."* He also said, *"I have a dream that my four little children will one day live in a nation where they will not be judged by the color of their skin but by the content of their character."* What are your thoughts on MLK's quotes?

147

There Are Good Cops

As you isolate well-meaning White anti-racist campaigners, you are also isolating the majority of police officers who do not kill people, nor are racists. Some more questions arise:

1. You mentioned very loudly that there are no good cops. So, the cops in the US and the UK who took the knee to respect the Black Lives Matter movement and honored George Floyd have no meaning. When police officers joined the BLM protests, you still consider them to be wrong. Why?

2. The Black retired police officer, David Dorn, was killed during the BLM protests by thugs who do not represent BLM. Was he a bad police officer?

3. When you blame all police officers for the sins of the few, you are doing precisely what White racists do when they blame all Black people for crimes and drugs or when anti-Muslim folks blame all Muslims for a few extremists who engage in terrorism. This is precisely how racists or prejudiced people think. And when we backtrack your thought process concerning the police, it is a biased outlook and runs parallel to your anti-White narrative. Do you still maintain that ALL police officers are bad? If so, then you are forced to admit that ALL Muslims are bad (terrorism) too. If not, what is the difference between the few rotten Muslim examples and the few horrible police officers?

4. Who will you call if a burglar or rapist breaks into your house? It was ironic when a Socialist Muslim activist in the US, Linda Sarsour, said that ALL police should be arrested

and supports their defunding. But then she put up a poster on Facebook from the NY Police Department appealing for witnesses to find a missing Muslim woman. So, who would you call upon to help you if you are a victim of a crime or witness a crime?

5. Police officers who have helped victims and saved lives, are they good or bad?

Burglary and Looting as Forms of Reparations

I had read somewhere on Medium.com that looting businesses and stealing food and clothes are reparations for slavery (not sure if it was one of your articles? I can't find it now). If you hold this view, then you are supporting criminal activity. Stealing or burning businesses does not compensate for slavery; it just teaches BAME children that you can steal. A few more points here:

1. A good argument in favor of reparations has come from a commentator who said that if slave owners were compensated for losing their slaves after abolition, and the last payment was made in 2015 (in the UK), then why don't victims deserve compensation? A good challenge back. I believe that the best form of reparations is freedom and equality. This is what MLK, Malcolm X, and other civil rights activists campaigned for. I am not aware of these activists demanding financial reparations for slavery.

2. Those who engaged in looting and violence have been condemned by BLM, by Terrence Floyd (George's brother), by Bernice King (daughter of MLK), and so on. Violence,

burning, and destruction are NOT in the DNA of Blacks nor BAME people. People may be from Antifa or White supremacists who posed as BLM activists and broke windows and destroyed buildings. While Black activists shouted at them to STOP. Yet your narrative (if you do support looting as a form of reparations) falls into the trap set by these White supremacists.

3. In the case of Indians, the best form of reparations they had because of British rule was an investment in India when it opened up to the world in the early 90s. The free market triggered the middle-class explosion, poverty elimination, technological development, and Indians now who are part of the British Government, making Britain decisions. The Indian subjects have broken free. They are starting to outperform their White ex-masters and take positions in the British administration, which was once occupied by White colonialists. To put the cherry on the cake, India will become a superpower within 20 years. This is the best form of reparation, by becoming successful, outdoing your ex-masters, and even ruling over them. Do you agree or disagree? If you disagree, then why?

4. How do I address the apparent contradiction in my argument where White slave owners were compensated for freeing slaves and that I do not advocate financial compensation to millions of African Americans, Africans, Indians, Malaysians, Indonesians, South Americans, Jews, etc.? There isn't enough money in the world economy to financially compensate around five billion people (I'm assuming there are five billion non-Whites). The best form of reparations is to make use of opportunities that are available today and excel. This is happening amongst Africans and Asians. Moreover, I don't believe that White slave owners should have been compensated.

5. How much should fifteen million Jews receive by Gentiles because they were massacred in the Holocaust and oppressed throughout history by Gentiles? They were also slaves under the Pharos thousands of years ago. What would reparations look like for this community?

6. As the anti-Capitalist narrative is quite strong within the Socialist movements and also within some infiltrators within BLM, they seek to exploit the murder of George Floyd to dismantle Capitalism and target large (and small) businesses. They want to bring down the very companies and their employees like myself, who are allies of BLM. Facebook, Walmart, and other large corporations have donated a total of 1 billion to BLM to ensure that racial injustices are erased. CEOs, managers, employees, and shareholders of these firms are allies of BLM, yet you are alienating once again. Goodyear's successful multinational corporation is a $15 billion company with global outreach across 64 countries employing 64,000 people and share prices increase on the NASDAQ after a dip. This is *Capitalism at its finest*. They went out of their way to support BLM and ban the support of '**Blue Lives Matter**' or '**All Lives Matter**' or '**MAGA**.' Yet many infiltrators within BLM would seek to destroy corporations like these. *Alienation at its finest*.

7. If the above arguments fail to convince you (apologies if you don't hold this view) that stealing and looting businesses is a form of reparation, please devise a strategy where reparations can occur. What will this look like? Let us start with Kamala Harris, whose ancestry traces back to Hamilton-Brown (through her father), who was a slave owner and owned more than 200 slaves. Her mother, Shymala Harris, boasted in an article that she is Brahmin by birth. The Indian caste system is a racist system that believes that people are born into castes. This is a misunderstanding and misuse of

Hinduism and the Vedic concept of the four castes (Brahmanas, Kshatriyas, Vaisyas, and Sudras). Caste (or different levels of being) is not a birth right as has been widely misunderstood. According to Vedic principles, they are determined by two things, Guna (quality) and Karma (the work you do). So, the work one does, and the type of human being determines how he progresses in society, i.e., his caste. But Shymala Harris's Brahmin supremacist and racist ideology, which has nothing to do with Vedic texts, needs to be challenged.

Let me make one thing clear. Kamala Harris is NOT responsible for her slave owner's forefather; neither is she accountable for her mother's racist views. But as a fighter against racism, the **starting** point for her has to be with her and her family. She should call out her mother for her racism; if Kamala does believe in reparations (I have not heard her state this, but let us assume this is a view you hold), then the starting point would be with her again. Her forefather, William Hamilton, benefited from slavery, and this benefit would have meandered down the generations through to today. So, given that Kamala is effectively a beneficiary of her forefather, what assets should she give up, and how much money should she donate? More importantly, to whom should she pay this?

CHAPTER 22

Conclusion

I hope you will take this response in the intended spirit, which is robust yet polite debate. I always enter a discussion or dialogue with the expectation that we learn from each other and that I could be wrong in my opinions and happy to change my views. I was educated only a few days ago when I read an article on Medium about Black men and the narrative that they are seen as criminals or incarcerated. The report states that Black men should not be perceived this way. They have responsibilities and are providers for their families. This did challenge me because I got sucked into the media narrative about Black men's incarcerations in the US. A new way of viewing them was an eye-opener.

I hope to have that experience when engaging with you as there will be gaps in my understanding of racism. As a Conservative, I have engaged with Socialists, feminists, pro-choice activists, Muslim extremists (when I stood for parliament in 2005, I challenged a Muslim extremist leader to debate after his group excommunicated me from Islam for standing for parliament. He chickened out), White supremacists, atheists, Jewish Rabbis, and Christian missionary friends. The conversations have always been respectful, and you will get the same respect from me even though we may disagree.

The only time I had a fallout was when I responded to a left wing socialist, feminist commentator in the UK when she criticized the Conservative Government for their handling of the COVID pandemic. I made the point-by-point rebuttals and expected a counter-response. Instead, she told me to delete my post and threatened to litigate if I did not. I did not. The explanation for this behavior is that she had a problem with a brown Conservative guy like me who dared to challenge a White feminist Socialist, something which she did not expect. When looking at your views about various groups have you have alienated White communities who are anti-racist?

You have alienated corporations and their employees and shareholders who have donated hundreds of millions of dollars to Black Lives Matter. Most Capitalist corporations and businesses are allies of BLM and funding anti-racist initiatives, only for some socialists within BLM. They seek to dismantle this very institution of Capitalism using the murder of George Floyd to advance their agenda. *Irony at its finest*.

You have alienated good police officers, including those who joined protesters and took the knee out to support the anti-racist cause.

You ignore racism within other communities. Have you alienated these groups, or have you alienated yourself by burning bridges instead of building them? Your philosophy is new and an interesting one, which seems to be anti-White racism.

I look forward to a positive engagement with you.

5) Re-thinking Donald Trump and the White Supremacy Narrative. Reflections on the Republican National Convention, Black Conservatives, and the Left's Latent Racism

A big shout to the Black Republican speakers at the RNC convention. I am sure that those on the far left will get angry when they see Black or brown speakers advocating a political philosophy pointing 180 degrees away from them. The reactions from well-meaning White folk on the left are always entertaining to watch; their racist reactions manifest themselves magnificently when they lecture BAME Conservatives that they are on the wrong side or token Blacks doing the bidding of White supremacy. It is the other way round. We are right to challenge many White folks on their privilege, which they may not be aware of. It is equally valid that well-meaning activists on the left, especially White activists, are unaware of their inherent racism when they feel anger towards Black and BAME Conservatives. They think that their non-White color should determine their preference for the Democrats in the US or Labour in the UK. I had witnessed this racist thinking when I got involved with the UK Conservative Party in the mid-1990s. I was told that Conservatives were racists, and that Labour was the party for Asians. The Liberal Democrats (UK's third party, which has very little influence) also played the race card with me when I stood for local elections in 2001. The left's inherent racist **conscious bias** out very well on five other occasions, as detailed below.

Left's Racism Par Excellence

Candace Owens. She an outspoken Black Conservative activist in the US. The White activists on the left hate her so much that one White woman tweeted a drawing of a White woman covering the mouth or a Black woman (who is meant to be Owens). The pictures are intended to convey that sometimes you need a White anti-racist activist to shut up a Black Conservative because she is a White supremacist. And the left cannot see the racism here. They are blind to their racism, just as many White folks are blind to their privilege—two sides of the same coin.

Dr. Stella Immanuel. When Donald Trump promoted a Black doctor, Stella Immanuel, there were criticisms of her wild views on demons. I subsequently came across a drawing of Trump consulting an African tribal voodoo witch doctor dressed in tribal gear and dancing. Those of you on the left side of politics, would this drawing seem funny? If so, then another introduction is to your latent racism; in the same way, many White folks have been introduced to their privilege.

Dismissal of BAME (Black, Asian, Minority Ethnic) Conservatives. Here in the UK, I listen to left commentators such as Kehinde Andrews, Afua Hirsh, and Nels Abbey. When the Conservative Government under Boris Johnson appointed the most diverse Cabinet historically, this went over these commentators' heads. Hirsh dismissed a Minister, Kemi Badenoch (from Nigeria), because she doesn't think Hirsh thought. Likewise, Andrews thought nothing much of Condoleezza Rice and criticized her for shoe shopping in New York when she should have been with President Bush during the Hurricane Katrina crisis. He avoided the fact that Rice called herself out for this mistake in her biography. He dismissed the numerous achievements she made as a high ranking and formidable adviser to President George W. Bush. This is the racism of groupthink, which is a peculiarity of the left.

My Own Experience: The UK Conservative Government's handling of the COVID pandemic had been mixed. There were successes, and there were failures. One Socialist feminist in the UK had written a post that went viral. She attacked the Government for some of its failures in the most ferocious manner. I responded in kind with a detailed outline of why she was wrong. She told me to take down my post; otherwise, she would launch litigation against me. My post is still up, and I am waiting for that litigation. What can explain this behavior? A White woman of the left could not handle a brown man on the right responding to every single charge.

Seeds of Anti-White Racism Being Planted: In another article on the publishing website, *Medium.com*, I wrote about my observation of a growing undercurrent of anti-White racism, as exemplified by the knee-on-neck incident where Isaiah Jackson placed his knee on a frightened two-year-old White toddler. The caption on the photo was '***BLM Now MF.***' There were no protests and no stern condemnation by groups supposedly protesting against racism. When I checked the social media pages of activists who had been strong in their condemnation of George Floyd's knee-on-neck incident, which led to his death, they

157

too were silent. I wrote to Black Lives Matter about their unusual silence. There were protests after the shooting of Jacob Blake, some of which had turned violent.

Unlike Floyd, Blake was a criminal with a warrant out for his arrest because of 3rd-degree sexual assault and carried a knife. Despite this, the shooting of Blake seven times is of concern, and it is natural for there to be anger and mass protests. Any person would be sympathetic to the ensuing peaceful demonstrations. Enter Cannon Hinnant. Do you know who he is? If not, why not? He was a five-year-old White boy who was shot dead in August by his neighbor, Darius Sessoms. This incident is more severe than Jacob Blake's ordeal. Yet I have not seen mass protests nor mass condemnation by activists on the left. Again, the Facebook pages of the activists were silent on this issue. Where was Reverend Al Sharpton to condemn this racist murder? Where was BLM?

Final Score: BAME – 1, White Privilege - 0

It is laughable that many folks on the left maintain that White privilege is a permanent fixture of Whiteness despite strides being made by BAME groups who are breaking through the ceiling and reaching a space once occupied by White privilege. I have yet to see a White politician from the UK's Labour Party who can match the Conservative Minister's intelligence and eruditeness, Kwasi Kwarteng, who is originally from Ghana. Their collective White privilege is no match for him. Let's take Rishi Sunak, who is the current British Finance Minister. His family is Hindus from India and Africa. He is an excellent Finance Minister who had a challenging task to kickstart the British economy during the coronavirus pandemic. He has been in a formidable position to make decisions and develop policies to do precisely that, thereby protecting jobs, livelihoods, and businesses in the

UK. When I read the transcript of the economic debate in Parliament on 8th July 2020 and compared the detailed plans of Sunak with the comments made by his opposition, Labour's Annaliese Dodds, the difference was like night and day. Her apparent White privilege came nowhere near Sunak's intellectual rigor and ability. How does the left deal with this? I consider Sunak to be in a superior (privileged?) position. Dodds is not. Deal with it. Own it.

The RNC Nuclear Blast - 2020

In 2016, I was horrified and disgusted with Trump during the primaries, and I remember the words of Marco Rubio that Trump was not a Conservative. Since Trump's election, I spoke on national radio condemning Trump about four times. Even as recent as 2019, I spent a few minutes on British national radio stating why Trump was a racist and not a Conservative. My discussion with the radio presenter, Shelagh Fogarty, can be accessed here:

https://youtu.be/dnkQH8tBofc

Now compare that discussion with my latest conversation with another radio presenter, Maajid Nawaz, on 29th August 2020:

https://www.youtube.com/watch?v=fvEuCBTVY0E&feature=youtu.be

One of the big surprises of the Republican National Convention was a list of policies enacted to empower Black communities, many of which I heard for the first time during the convention. If anyone should be angry with many of Trump's policies designed to help Black communities, it is White supremacists. The policies I am referring to are as follows:

1. **Increase in job creation** before COVID-19.

2. **Increase in and permanent funding of Black universities.**

I heard this at the RNC in 2020, when the executive order to enact this funding took place in 2017. I was unaware of this. I just located a video on this executive order here:

https://www.youtube.com/watch?v=U-wqUuEM3Lg

3. **Reduction in incarcerations through the First Step Act.**

It was good to see the Black grandmother, Alice Johnson, pardoned by Trump, and she was one of the speakers at the RNC. Although CNN's Jake Tapper did state that Trump told 20 lies during his speech, he was open enough to invite Alice Johnson for an interview, and she lauded Trump's pardon of her crime. Respect to Jake Tapper and CNN!

4. **Trump's staunch pro-life stance.**

I wasn't aware of it. He mentioned his pro-Life stance in passing during his debate with Hillary Clinton in 2016, but I wasn't aware of the policies he enacted to reduce abortions. What has this got to do with helping Black communities? More Black babies are aborted proportionately than White babies in the US. I have described myself as a Conservative ally of Black Lives Matter (BLM) and that everyone should be an ally. I still maintain this despite the rioters and terrorists who have infiltrated this movement. I have no hesitation in pushing back and challenging BLM to change their slogan from 'BLM' to 'ABLM' (ALL Black Lives Matter). This includes unborn Black babies. If there is push-back from feminists and BLM, the right to choose abortions is sacred and that this principle is the pinnacle of civilization and human greatness; my counter push back would be, *'WHY don't ALL Black lives matter?'* That's a debate for another time. No. Let's debate this now. If this critical debate does not take off now, I expect the next generation to take the mantle. Just as we have been encouraged to have courageous conversations with the older generation about their racism and to call them out at the dinner table, I expect the next generation to have courageous conversations with us and challenge us at the dinner table on why we didn't do anything to correct the most heinous injustices being carried out against innocent lives.

5. **The School Choice Program**.

I heard about this policy about three weeks ago when Condoleezza Rice mentioned it. This initiative gives children from low-income families, including many Black families, the chance to go to those private schools parents would like to see their children get an education from. This is the 'pro-choice' thing I am talking about. I favor this initiative because this is precisely what the UK Conservatives did in the 1990s under Prime Minister John Major through the Assisted Places Scheme; poor parents of bright children would receive vouchers to send their children to private schools choice. Many low-income families benefited, including a friend who explained how the scheme helped him. He is prosperous today. Unfortunately, the Labour Party dismantled the plan when they came to power in 1997. An absolute travesty and an attack on low-income families. It is good to know that the School Choice Program is getting traction in the US under Trump.

6. **Helping Black Business Owners.**

This was not mentioned in the RNC, but I found this video clip from another source (Timestamp 7:45).

https://www.youtube.com/watch?v=jJp4xXDFkho&t

Trump offered to help business owners, including a Black business owner whose business was destroyed during the protests by thugs and bandits who used the cover BLM's peaceful protests to enact these wanton acts of violence. It doesn't help BLM's cause when one of its officials, Ariel Atkins, said that burning businesses is ok because it is payback for slavery and that these companies will receive insurance checks. BLM as an organization that does NOT advocate violence, which is why they should condemn these incitements to violence. Moreover, I am always amazed how people like Ariel Atkins and Tamika Mallory dare to deliver veiled criticisms of George Floyd's family and Bernice King (daughter of Martin Luther King Jr.) and other Black folks who have condemned the use of violence. MLK was evident in why non-violence was the best approach, and he won. That the Ariels and Tamikas of the far left would shamelessly dare to try to prove MLK wrong is beyond reprehensible. BLM needs to recognize that it can no longer be held hostage by thugs on the far left (with the help of White supremacists and Antifa agitators who had broken buildings when Black protesters pleaded with them to stop). BLM needs to purge these violent agitators so that protests can be peaceful once again.

7. **Trump About to Knock out a KKK Supporter in 2016.**

This incident happened, not at the RNC 2020, but a Trump rally in 2016. Just to put the icing on the cake of the link between White supremacy and Donald Trump, I had heard of David Duke endorsing Trump. I never understood why Trump was silent on the matter, and it compounded my narrative of Trump being in bed with a racist. But I discovered only a few days ago exactly what Trump thinks of the KKK. CNN's video here:

https://www.youtube.com/watch?v=1evyptWWgDE

This video shows the clip of a KKK member supporting Trump. Trump eyeballed him and looked like he was about to knock him out WWE style. He even complained about why the police did not eject him. Trump also condemned David Duke and the KKK by name in 2016. According to CNN, he said, "David Duke is a bad person, who I disavowed on numerous occasions over the years," Trump said on MSNBC's *Morning Joe.* "I disavowed him. I disavowed the KKK," Trump added. "Do you want me to do it again for the 12th time? I disavowed him in the past, I disavow him now." (CNN website, 3rd March 2016)

Is the Media to Blame?

I wasn't aware of the above policies or facts even though I watched CNN and CNBC for a while. Either I don't get out much, or there was little coverage of the points mentioned above. I have always held CNN with high regard as a formidable broadcaster. I do like to watch Don Lemon, Jake Tapper, Anderson Cooper, and Christiane Amanpour. Fox News was taken off the air in the UK. But if I did have access, then I would listen to Laura Ingraham and Tucker Carlson, although I don't like Carlson's continuous high carb attacks on the Democrats. Unfortunately, I had to learn about Black speakers' actual pro-Black policies at a Republican Convention a few years after some of these policies were enacted. Should I blame the media? I don't know. I don't like playing the media blame game.

Confusion About Trump

I did watch part of the Democrat National Convention coverage the week before. It was a relatively good convention with a good line-up of speakers. When I heard Conservative speakers like Colin Powell and John Kasich speak on the DNC platform, I sympathized with them. But then came the Republican National Convention's nuclear blast, which got me into a head-spin. I remain unclear on one thing. If Trump's policies mentioned above have empowered Black communities, why are notable doyens of the Republican Party (Powell, Kasich, Bush, Romney) supporting Biden? Whatever the explanation, I know this. The RNC outdid the DNC. I don't know how to read Trump now. But I know how to read our activist friends on the left and far left. They will hate the Black conservative speakers for daring to step out of the Democrat '*plantation*.' This is misdirected hate and misfiring of anger. These emotions should come from the far right White supremacists who would be loathing Trump for his pro-Black policies, but they are coming from a direction which one would least expect. It shows that racism is alive and well among the far left, especially among its White activists and White supremacists on the far right.

Confusion About the Democrats and the Left

While I am on the topic of 'confusion,' let me slip in two things that have been bothering me.

1. The "MeToo" Movement.

The experiences of women who were victims of sexual harassment were highlighted a couple of years ago during the Brett Kavanaugh and Christine Ford hearings. There was a movement of women victims to come out and share their painful stories. It was a good cause, and I supported its objectives. The Women's March, led by Linda Sarsour, protested against Kavanaugh and supported Ford. Many will recall Kamala Harris telling Ford, '*I believe you.*' They will also remember the incident when Linda Sarsour burst into Kavanaugh's session to protest against him. Two years later, when there is a charge of sexual harassment against Joe Biden based on more substantial evidence than Christine Ford's account, stunned silence. Where are the protests now against sexual harassment? Democrats, including Kamala Harris, have dishonored the "MeToo" movement and reversed its good cause and the good reputation it built over the last two years.

2. Racism Shown by Joe Biden.

In another article, I stated that Joe Biden was evident in his racism when he told Black voters that they were not Black if they could not decide between Trump and Biden. Discrimination is as clear as daylight. But I guess Biden is Biden, so the left chooses to let him off. During the primaries, Kamala Harris tore into Biden and made a veiled accusation against Biden for supporting segregation in busing. She was very serious about her charge, only to minimize its impact a year later when she told Stephen Colbert that it was only a 'debate.'

Here is the confusion. How is it possible for Kamala Harris (and the Democrats), who was outspoken and vociferous against Brett Kavanaugh, and equally vicious against Joe Biden's support of segregationists, only to support an alleged rapist and racist? It seems that principles don't matter anymore because the quest for power is the end game. They are willing to ditch the "MeToo" movement and overlook racism within their own ranks when they see the highest office in the land within striking distance. Imagine my disappointment when I learn that the US's left is a mirror image of the UK's left. I thought Americans were more sophisticated. Not. I have seen how the left in the UK use BAME people and the feminist narrative to achieve their agenda, only to ditch them when they are no longer needed. Democrats can be better than that.

There is one thing about the Democrats I am not confused about, but the younger generation might be. In the Democrats' website, the 'Our History' section quotes the following statement, *'For more than 200 years, our party has led the fight for civil rights, health care, Social Security, workers' rights, and women's rights. We are the party of Barack Obama, John F. Kennedy, FDR, and the countless everyday Americans who work each day to build a perfect union.'* I had a slight smile. The history seems to start from the early 20th Century.

So, what happened to the previous 100 years? Democrats were the party of slavery, segregation, lynching, and the KKK. The party of Jim Crow and Stephen Douglas. Why isn't the abolition of slavery a part of the history of the Democrats? Because they did not abolish it, they supported it. I only discovered this fact as recently as 2018 when I thought I had figured out American politics. If I was in the dark for so long after I became 'aware' of American politics during the Bush-Dukakis Presidential Election in 1988, then how many more young Democrats are living in ignorance? The Democrats website will not fully furnish their 200-year history. Their history starts from the 20th Century, and the previous sordid period has been magically erased. The new narrative is that Donald Trump is racist.

Stephen Douglas put forward a magnificent defense of slavery during the Lincoln-Douglas debates. Douglas's arguments were from a 'pro-choice' perspective (sound familiar?). The Republican Party is the party of Abraham Lincoln and abolitionists. It was created for the sole purpose of abolishing slavery and campaigned in subsequent civil rights movements. To the Republicans, Black lives mattered too much, which is why they fought the Democrats to cancel it, and Abraham Lincoln was assassinated for it by a Confederate/Democrat. Although Trump mentioned Lincoln in his RNC speech, he missed out on the crucial element of the Republican Party's foundation. Even if things go wrong for the Republicans, they have a proud history and a strong foundation to build on. Democrats don't. That will never change.

Some Good Policies of the Democrats

As a reasonable Conservative, I don't dismiss everything, Democrat. If I were American, I would have voted for Hillary Clinton in 2016 because I could not stand Trump based on misplaced stereotypes. I agree with the Democrats on their policy on universal healthcare. Hillary Clinton tried to develop a health service that was free for all Americans. That failed because of recalcitrant politicking from the Republicans. All political parties in the UK support the British Health Service (NHS), a universal healthcare system. Despite pressures on the NHS, its service is first class and is our national treasure. I am surprised that the most powerful and advanced nation on earth doesn't have universal healthcare, although it has universal education.

I also agree with their stance on gun control and restricting access. The British/European countries do not allow guns, even by the police (except for the armed units), Americans do. There is a cultural difference that is directing me more towards the Democrat stance on guns.

The Hope of a Civil Discourse

As I witness the genesis of a civil war inside the US after the murder of George Floyd and the shooting of Jacob Blake, it is incumbent upon Trump and Biden to use their positions of power to try to unite the country rather than play the divisive politics, which has been plaguing America. I was very interested in the actual policies that Trump had implemented for Black America, which I hadn't heard about before. During the Presidential debates, the Trump card that Trump should be playing is the focus on actual achievements for the economy, Black employment (pre-COVID), funding of Black universities, reduce incarcerations of Black prisoners, etc. because this is the only platform which voters will get to hear about these policies.

The main media outlets will not shout about them, and Democrats will do everything they can to put a lid on these concrete achievements; instead, they may focus on Trump's mishandling of the pandemic, they will surely blame the riots and anarchy on the office of the presidency and will concentrate on embarrassing gaffs made by Trump. Biden has sounded out these diversionary tactics by blaming Trump for riots in Portland and Minneapolis but did not bother blaming Obama for the Baltimore riots in 2015. Work that one out. Trump is too volatile to stick with concrete policies during Presidential debates. Hence, I think that both septuagenarians will probably be comparing their dick sizes more than anything else. Biden will attack Trump's volatile personality and numerous silly statements he made. Trump will exploit Biden's cognitive decline. America won't be great at that moment in time.

More traction might be observed during the Vice-Presidential debate. This will be of interest because I know about Kamala Harris's strengths and weaknesses regarding policies and principles, but I know very little about Mike Pence. Could he land a surprise in the same way the RNC 2020 did? Let's wait and see. I hope they display the same level of civility I saw between Dick Cheney and Joe Liberman during the Vice-Presidential debate in 2000.

I may retract the accusation of racism against Trump, which I made over the last few years. Actions speak louder than words. And his efforts that helped Black communities resounded. Nevertheless, Trump remains an enigma. But Black Lives Matter remains a bigger enigma because they refuse to call out violent protestors who hide behind its good name and peaceful message and refuse to condemn blatant anti-White racism and abortion of Black babies (ALL Black lives matter…. remember? If you disagree, then you have no right to call out the older generation at the dinner table, for their past racism).

Black Lives Matter – Black Breakthrough Matters More

I am a Conservative ally of Black Lives Matter, but I am running on fumes. It is inspirational leaders like Donovan Livingston which makes me remain an ally. I first came across Livingston a few days ago when his graduation speech at Harvard University came into my timeline. He gave his speech in 2016, but I only saw it recently by accident. It was the BEST speech I have heard since George Floyd's death. No other politician nor activist has been able to inspire the way he did four years ago. His power of oration and the use of poetry to light fires in the hearts of people was incredible. I told my 9-year-old daughter to finish her dinner so that I could show his speech to her. **Everyone** should listen to his wise words and moments of inspiration. He is a part of BLM, but his peaceful, yet powerful messages are drowned out by the violence of thugs and rioters who have hijacked BLM.

Donovan Livingston Speech – Harvard 2016:

https://www.youtube.com/watch?v=9XGUpKITeJM&t

Other inspirational speeches by inspirational Black speakers from Harvard are listed below.

Jonathan Roberts Speech – Harvard 2017

https://www.youtube.com/watch?v=gBkcFjS9asc

Eunice Mwabe Speech – Harvard 2019

https://www.youtube.com/watch?v=3j7BYyR93WQ

Welcome to '**Black Breakthrough,**' where White privilege is only a mirage. While everyone should remember the injustices against George Floyd, Breonna Taylor, Ahmad Arbery, etc. and bring police officers to justice, Black America should **never be solely** linked with slavery, racism, and police brutality. This paints a false narrative that their future will always be in chains. BAME people are breaking through the stereotypes by achieving success. The only groups whose interest it serves to keep the stereotype of constant racism and brutality of Blacks are the left. It is easier to control the masses when they are in a state of rage, anger, and shock. I am beginning to see what the Black Republican speakers meant when they said they have broken out of the Democrat plantation and have become free thinkers. There is still hope in America.

My parting message to Donovan Livingstone is this, '*reach the stars brother, and let your words of peace, courage, and hope, purge the gaslighting of America. You are America's last hope, Mr. Future President.*'

Postscript

At the time of this book's publication, President Trump selected Amy Coney Barrett to be on the Supreme Court. The first presidential debate took place between Trump and Biden. Trump was then diagnosed with COVID-19 and subsequently discharged from the hospital after being treated. The mainstream media, such as CNN, criticized Trump for his selection of Amy Barrett, his bluster during the debate, and being irresponsible by getting discharged from the hospital early. We don't get Fox News in the UK; hence, CNN is my only source of Americana on TV. How do I make sense of all this? And what is my view of Trump now after mentioning him only once, where I criticized him in the main part of the book, followed by a subsequent article where I seem to have had a change of heart?

A) First Presidential Debate

What a debacle. As I predicted, Trump lambasted Biden and interrupted him frequently. The moderator, Chris Wallace, ended up trying to control Trump and even became his second opponent. America was not great at that time. And the world would have been laughing. Ardent Trump supporters praised him for his boisterous approach, while Biden supporters and the mainstream media (CNN) slated Trump for his poor behavior.

The debate platform was a missed opportunity for Trump to lay out his policies that empowered black communities through increased employment, lower incarcerations, and extended funding for back universities. His 'School Choice' program for schools is a good policy to empower parents to send their children to private schools. Many manufacturing jobs came back to America. He presided over two peace deals between Israel, UAE and Bahrain. The success of the ongoing Middle East Peace process is unprecedented. The economy was performing better pre-COVID. His pro-life stance is quite strong. Instead, Trump's bluster towards Biden overshadowed these policy achievements.

In contrast, Biden did better than expected. Before the debate, I revisited his previous debates with Sarah Palin in 2008 and Paul Ryan in 2012. He performed strongly and assertively in contrast to recent speeches and interviews where his cognitive decline was apparent. I feared that Trump would exploit this weakness in his opponent. However, Trump's tornado-like bluster only angered Biden, which made him more alert and coherent! Trump's volatile behavior was easy fodder for his opponents in the media. If he had stuck to his policy achievements and his smart come-backs instead of continuous interruptions, the debate would have taken a different turn. The reader probably thinks that I may as well be on Trump's campaign team. No, thank you, I have not made up my mind about Trump yet.

Let's hope that subsequent Presidential debates are more amicable and meaningful in contrast to the septuagenarians comparing their sizes.

B) The President's Covid-19 Diagnosis – Triumphant Trump?

I have not looked into Trump's handling of the COVID pandemic. I have heard of many criticisms of his alleged mishandling of the situation. When I heard of Trump's diagnosis, it reminded me of Prime Minister Boris Johnson's COVID diagnosis a few months ago. It brought home the seriousness of the pandemic. Prayers were sent to Johnson, in the same way prayers were sent to Trump by friends and foe alike. The mainstream Democrats sent their best wishes. This is how opponents and adversaries are meant to behave. However, some far left commentators hoped that Trump would die. When I checked the social media pages of an American Socialist organization, the message board was replete with messages of death and damnation for Trump. Again, not surprising.

When the British ex-Prime Minister, Margaret Thatcher, died in 2013, there was jubilation from Socialists and far left groups. They do this. It's in their nature. It's part of the program. Ignore them. I was glad when Trump showed improvements, and I was also glad that Joe Biden tested negative. I wish both well, and so should the reader. Linda Sarsour was ambivalent. When she posted Trump's tweet on the 5th of October 2020, about him feeling better, her only comment was, **'Lord help us.'** I am sure she meant that he should have stayed back in the hospital to recover. I won't read into it any further.

Knowing what I know about Trump's narcissism, if he fully pulls through, this would be seen as a massive victory for him. Trump came face to face with the virus, and he triumphed. The political currency that would be gained is phenomenal this close to the election. He's been there, done that, and worn the T-shirt. He is likely to say that if he has been able to pull through, then only he would know best how to pull America out of this pandemic. I am sure his campaign managers are working overtime to create a superhero (just replace the 'S' symbol in the Superman costume with a 'T').

What has been very peculiar about the reporting of the COVID pandemic in the American and British media is that when protests were in full force after George Floyd's tragic murder, hundreds of thousands of BAME protesters took to the streets during the height of the pandemic during the lockdown in the US and the UK. It is a medical fact that BAME people are at higher risk of being adversely affected by COVID-19. In the book, I mentioned that there were White agitators who may have been from Antifa or White supremacists, who destroyed buildings and may have engineered BAME people's anger to get them out onto the streets and expose themselves to further risk. Thus, the Coronavirus would have been turbocharged, and the victims would be the BAME protesters, many of whom were not wearing masks. The various media outlets did not report on this increased risk to the BAME protesters. However, COVID-19 became an issue in the media when Trump supporters gathered in Trump events, and there were talks of these supporters increasing their risks to COVID-19 exposure. Both the protests and the Trump campaigns took place around the same time, yet the media was silent on the issue of COVID-19 risk to BAME folks who were out in force. I cannot explain this divergence in reporting.

C) *The Grave Charge of White Supremacy and Fascism*

A peculiar charge against Trump is 'white supremacist' or 'Fascist.' He had failed to condemn White supremacy in the strongest terms during the Presidential debate, his one-word answer, 'sure' did not placate the questioner. This was seen as proof that Trump was a racist and a White supremacist. This charge is quite rich, given that he had developed policies to empower Black America. The question should be redirected to White supremacy organizations. They should be asked what they think of Trump's pro-Black, pro-Latino policies. They will dissociate themselves from Trump. White racists and Fascists do NOT empower Black or BAME communities. The Press Secretary, Kayleigh McEnany, listed a series of Trump's historical quotes condemning racism and White supremacy. The Federal execution of the White supremacist, Daniel Lewis Lee, in July was performed under the Trump presidency. While the criticism of Trump's lame condemnation of White supremacy during the debate is justified, for some reason, his other quotes condemning white supremacy were ignored. The execution of Danie Lewis Lee meant nothing. Trump is still a racist. Two questions come to mind:

1. If racism is so important (which it is), why have Democrats ignored the racist statement made by Biden, that if Blacks cannot decide whether to vote for Trump or not, then they ain't Black? Not to mention the serious accusation of racism made by Kamala Harris during the Democrat Primaries?

2. White supremacy and racism are among the worst violations of human rights. We can also agree that sexual assault is on par with this gross injustice. Tara Reade --

remember? Why are many media outlets and feminists, and the #MeToo movement silent on this alleged crime?

It seems that if left commentators and activists do not like someone, they will charge them with White supremacy or something similar. Amy Barrett is a case in point. A formidable and able woman has been selected to be a judge on the Supreme Court. It seems that feminists, who campaign for more empowerment of women, agree with women's empowerment up to a point. If the woman in question is a Conservative or is religious (in this case she belongs to, 'People of Praise' a sect of the Catholic Church) or is pro-Life, then the advocacy for female empowerment stops. This is not surprising. We had the same experience here in the UK. Margaret Thatcher became the first British woman Prime Minister in 1979, who transformed the socio-economic landscape of Britain for the better. She was hated by many women/feminists on the left because of the divergence in their political ideologies.

XX-chromosomes only matter if the ideology of the owner of these chromosomes is left-leaning. How is Amy Barrett connected to White supremacy? She has many children, two of whom are adopted Black children from Haiti. Hateful critics of Barrett charge her with White colonialism because she adopted Black children in order to instil 'superior' White values. The left's 'art of the spin' is remarkable. I recall Hollywood stars who also adopted Black babies, not receiving this charge of White colonialism. Barrett and her family treat the two Black kids as their own and are equal. The left will not see the Black kids as being equal with her family; hence racism exudes from their thought patterns. Their racism (or White supremacy?) is further exposed when we ask the question, '*why would left critics consider the white family as superior colonialists, but not entertain the possibility that the black children come from a superior culture?'*

This is about keeping Black and BAME communities down there at an inferior level. When we are down there, despondent and angry, then it is easier to manipulate us.

My book has engaged the reader with a few thought experiments. Consider the following as the final thought experiment. You have a couple. One of the spouses is White, and the other is non-White. I have seen many couples that are mixed race. I am sure you have too. Has it ever occurred to you that the White husband or wife ever considered themselves as superior to their non-White spouses? Or that the reason for marrying them or going out with them is to instill 'civilized White values?' Did the non-White spouse (let's say husband) ever think that he got married to his White wife because he felt inferior and needed some White colonialism or did they just love each other and wanted to make a life together? I once had a conversation with a White female colleague who told me she did have a Black boyfriend, and there were talks of marriage. But both she and her boyfriend had negative comments from their respective families and friends. I told her that she should have gone for it and not worry about what others would say. Looking back at this conversation, it did not occur to me nor to her nor to her Black boyfriend that she intended to impart White colonialism to him!

It seems that the charge of White colonialism does not apply to couples who marry or go out with each other, but does apply when a strong, loving Conservative Christian family wants to adopt children from different cultures to give them better lives by being a part of their family. The psychological thought process is amazing yet bewildering.

Readers may recall one of the Black Conservative speakers at the RNC, Daniel Cameron. He said, *"Whether you are the family of Breonna Taylor or David Dorn, these are the ideals that will heal our nation's wounds," he said. "Republicans will never turn a blind eye to unjust acts."*

I noticed that he received a lot of criticism for using the name 'Breonna Taylor.' Why? Because Taylor belongs to the left, who have been campaigning to bring police officers to justice for her killing. They have made Taylor their own, and for a Black Conservative speaker to mention her name in a national Republican convention seems sacrilege. Cameron was right to mention Taylor AND David Dorn. Dorn was a retired black police officer who was killed during a protest, yet his name does not appear in the left's narrative. It seems they own Breonna Taylor, Ahmaud Arberry, Rayshard Brooks, etc. And if any Conservative dares to mention their names in the context of justice and peace, they will be lambasted because it's not their turf. **No one owns anyone.** Slavery was abolished in 1865 by the Republicans while facing fierce opposition from the old Democrats.

'Fascism,' 'racism,' and 'White supremacy' should not be used as political footballs just because the activists on the left hate Trump. This would be a grave dishonor to the victims of such evil ideologies, and their suffering is used to make political capital is abhorrent.

D) Dialogue with a Liberal about Trump's Apparent Fascism

I came across an article by Kitanya Harrison, who posed the question in her title, *"Should You Wish a Fascist Well?"* I responded with the following:

I would be interested to know why Trump is a Fascist? As far as I know, Fascists and racists do not extend funding for Black universities, nor do they lower the incarceration rates of Black men (1994 Crime Bill) or improve Black communities' job prospects, pre-COVID. Trump is a racist or Fascist because....?

When Biden said that you ain't Black if you can't choose whether to vote for Trump or not; or when Kamala Harris lambasted Biden for his racism around the issue of busing, Biden is not a racist because…?

Reply from 'Larry' — A Commentator

As I mentioned earlier in response to another's comment, it has a good definition of Fascism based on Umberto Ecco and Lawrence Britt's work:

http://www.rense.com/general37/char.htm

When you look at these 14 points, Trump does come across as a classic fascist in the same mold as Galtieri, Mussolini, Berluscone, Peron, and Franco.

My Reply

Many thanks, Larry. I have read your comments to other article writers and commentators. I understand you are a scientist, which is great. I look forward to engaging with someone like yourself, who has critical thinking at his disposal. I have looked at the 14 criteria for Fascism, set out in the Liberty Forum by Dr. Lawrence Britt when he examined the Fascist regimes of Hitler (Germany), Mussolini (Italy), Franco (Spain), Suharto (Indonesia), and several Latin American regimes. These would be my responses as someone who is not a Trump supporter yet:

1. Powerful and Continuing Nationalism — Fascist regimes tend to make constant use of patriotic mottos, slogans, symbols, songs, and other paraphernalia. Flags are seen everywhere, as are flag symbols on clothing and in public displays.

Reply: Flags and symbols do appear in Socialist or Communist regimes too. Flag symbolism and patriotism are universal. I have seen Democrats and Republicans use the American flag as a sense of pride. During the general elections in the UK, the left-leaning Labour Party used the British flag in their conventions; so did our Party (Conservative Party). The Soviet Union took pride in their flag, as does China. They were or are Communist/Socialist in political structure, although the economies now are Capitalist. Flag-waving and symbols are not the only remits of Fascists. So, why is Trump an outlier here?

2. Disdain for the Recognition of Human Rights — Because of fear of enemies and the need for security, the people in fascist regimes are persuaded that human rights can be ignored in certain cases because of "need." The people tend to look the other way or even approve of torture, summary executions, assassinations, long incarcerations of prisoners, etc.

Reply: Human rights violations are universal, unfortunately. I have not heard Trump say that human rights can be ignored. A recent Federal execution that did take place under Trump's administration was of the white supremacist murderer, Daniel Lewis Lee. Do you agree or disagree with this? With regard to incarcerations, Trump did reduce incarcerations of Black men. Bill Clinton did admit that the 1994 Crime Bill (which led to increased incarcerations of black men) was a mistake. As far as I know, President Trump has not ordered any assassinations other than Al-Baghdadi, the ISIS leader.

Let's not forget that President Obama had Bin Laden killed too. Obama has never been described as a Fascist, so why is Trump when you consider the above?

3. Identification of Enemies/Scapegoats as a Unifying Cause — The people are rallied into a unifying patriotic frenzy over the need to eliminate a perceived common threat or foe: racial, ethnic or religious minorities; liberals; communists; socialists, terrorists, etc.

Reply: When did Trump say that ethnic or religious minorities were enemies? He did condemn terrorists (e.g., ISIS, Al-Qaeda, extremism), but so did Obama, Bush, Clinton, etc. The fact that Communists or Socialists are treated as foes is not unique to Trump. America, under the Democrats and Republicans, has always competed with the USSR and Communism. The Democrat President, J. F. Kennedy, nearly went to war with the USSR during the Cuban Missile Crisis in the 1960s. Did Kennedy have Fascistic tendencies because of his imminent threat to the Soviet Union? Even the UK under Conservative's Margaret Thatcher and under Labour's Tony Blair was not considered Fascist, even though they were anti-Socialist. Tony Blair dumped a lot of his party's Socialist principles to get elected in 1997. Was he a Fascist? No. So, why is Trump an outlier here?

Let us not have collective amnesia about Vladimir Lenin and his *'Red Terror'* campaign against his opponents in the USSR during the Russian civil war in 1918, where state security services were used as part of the repression. A propaganda poster stated, *"Death to the Bourgeoisie and its lapdogs. Long live Red Terror."* Lenin's successor, Joseph Stalin had his own version of Marxism when he, too, unleashed a campaign of terror known as the *'Great Purge'* and *'Dekulakization,'* which saw executions, mass arrests, religious persecution, forced labor, and concentration camps known as '*gulags.*'

Fascism and Communism/Marxism/Stalinism seem to be two sides of the same coin.

4. Supremacy of the Military — Even when there are widespread domestic problems, the military is given a disproportionate amount of government funding, and the domestic agenda is neglected. Soldiers and military service are glamorized.

Reply: Creating a strong military is not just the remit of Fascist states. Hitler, Mussolini, Galtieri, etc. were mentioned at the beginning. Surprisingly, Lenin and Stalin were not mentioned. As mentioned in no. 3 above, they, too, were dictators and had a strong military and security apparatus. The Soviet Union had massive military firepower and became one of the global superpowers because of it in the late 20th Century. China and India are on their way to achieving military might. Are they Fascist states? You may recall the five-day 'Vostok 2018' military exercises between Russia and China, which was bigger than 'Zapad 81', where the USSR engaged in massive military maneuvers in Eastern Europe in 1981. They sent a clear message to the US of their military might. Ok, they were boys playing with their big toys to show off their muscles. Vostok 2018 showcased the Russian-Chinese military prowess, but I never heard of them being described Fascist. I am not indicating that you support Socialism or Communism. In fact, you had criticized the Soviet propaganda machine when they used 'whataboutery' to justify their controversial actions.

On the 20th of September 2020, Trump accused military generals of wanting to fight wars to keep weapons manufacturers happy. He clashed with Pentagon leaders. He also started pulling out troops from Iraq and Afghanistan. As far as I know, he did not start a new war. Previous Democrat and Republican presidents did preside over controversial wars. Soldiers and military personnel are treated as heroes by all parties in all countries. In fact, during the Presidential debate when Joe Biden mentioned his late son, Bau, who served in the military, Trump should have thanked Bau for his services. Praising the sacrifice that soldiers make in their line of duty is not Fascism. Every year on the 11th hour of the 11th day of the 11th month (November), Armistice Day is observed in the UK, which commemorates fallen soldiers during World War 1. Two minutes of silence is observed. VE (Victory in Europe) Day is also celebrated in relation to World War II. The fallen soldiers are not glamorized; they are respected because they sacrificed their lives to combat Fascism. How does Trump fit in to point no. 4?

5. Rampant Sexism — The governments of fascist nations tend to be almost exclusively male-dominated. Under fascist regimes, traditional gender roles are made more rigid. Divorce, abortion and homosexuality are suppressed, and the state is represented as the ultimate guardian of the family institution.

Reply: I agree with the abortion bit. But being Pro-Life is not a Fascist ideology. It is to do with the abuse of human rights (point no. 2 above). Leaving this aside, where did Trump suppress divorce or homosexuality? Conservatives believe in minimal state interference. So, the state would not guard the family institution; communities would. And what is wrong with the family institution? Why is this Fascist? How does Trump fit into all this? Speaking of sexism, you will agree that sexual harassment and abuse are the worst forms of sexism that men can inflict on women. I take the point that Trump was awful in 2005 when he told Billy Bush that he would like to grab the private part of the actress, Arianne

Zucker. Here is the problem. Trump fantasized in 2005 what Joe Biden did in 1993 when he allegedly penetrated Tara Reade with his fingers. Let's call this 'digital rape.' There is stoned silence among the Democrats on this issue, who are not supporting Tara Reade, and have certainly let down Christine Blasey Ford by ditching her after the Kavanaugh hearings in 2019. Using no. 5 as a criterion, then the charge of Fascism applies to Biden more than it does to Trump. Why is Trump an outlier here?

6. Controlled Mass Media — Sometimes to media is directly controlled by the government, but in other cases, the media is indirectly controlled by government regulation or sympathetic media spokespeople and executives. Censorship, especially in wartime, is very common.

Reply: How and where does Trump control the mass media? CNN and CNBC are the only American channels we get in the UK (and C-Span for a few hours on Sunday). Fox News was taken off the air a few years ago after Rupert Murdoch sold Sky TV. When I watch CNN, it is replete with anti-Trump opinions. If Trump controlled the mass media, why hasn't he shut down CNN and arrest Jake Tapper, Don Lemon, Chris Cuomo, and Erin Burnett, who continuously accuse Trump of lying? He does not control the media. But rather, the media can manipulate opinion (whether the right or left) and is not under the President's control. How does Trump control mass media and censor them?

7. Obsession with National Security — Fear is used as a motivational tool by the government over the masses.

Reply: National Security and fear may go hand in hand. But National Security became important after the 9/11 attacks under President Bush and his adviser, Condolezza Rice. Were they Fascists? Why hasn't the USSR or China been mentioned as having extensive and formidable security apparatus? Why is Trump an outlier here?

8. Religion and Government are Intertwined — Governments in fascist nations tend to use the most common religion in the nation as a tool to manipulate public opinion. Religious rhetoric and terminology are common from government leaders, even when the major tenets of the religion are diametrically opposed to the government's policies or actions.

Reply: The US Constitution gives rights to all religions. Having a Christian foundation as laid out by the Founding Fathers, no Christian sect has priority over another. America was founded on the principle that God's Providence does not come through the British Royal Family; it comes directly to people. Judeo-Christian values (in parallel with Islamic values and similar values from other faiths) are America's foundations. This does not mean Fascism unless you imply that God is a Fascist. God is certainly not a Marxist because Karl Marx opined that religion was the opiate of the masses. All American Presidents have chanted, 'God Bless America.' I recall Barack Obama quoting a passage from the Bible a few years ago. They are not Fascists, so why is Trump, in the context of religion? What are your thoughts on the USSR promoting Atheism and oppressing religious minorities? Or China's oppression of the Uighur Muslims? Those states are not Fascists, so how do we describe them? This is not Soviet-style 'whataboutery;' I am highlighting a contradiction in your line of thinking.

9. Corporate Power is Protected — The industrial and business aristocracy of a fascist nation often are the ones who put the government leaders into power, creating a mutually beneficial business/government relationship and power elite.

Reply: Which business or industry put Trump in the White House? If I recall, he put up his own money during the 2016 campaign. Business relations with the government are not a function of Fascism. The (South) Korean business conglomerates known as 'Chaebols' had very close ties with the government. Both benefited. Now, many Korean firms have become successful multinationals. South Korea is a rising tiger nation and a success story. Where does Fascism fit in? The irony of ironies is this. The far left activists want to bring down the very Capitalist corporations that donated $1 billion to combat racism in the US. I would like to know how the money has been spent. If criteria no. 9 insinuates that Capitalist corporations are the problem here, how are they linked to Fascism? Capitalist corporations have donated money to the Republicans and Democrats. Should both parties, therefore, be classified as Fascists? Which business aristocracy made Trump President?

10. Labor Power is Suppressed — Because the organizing power of labor is the only real threat to a fascist government, labor unions are either eliminated entirely, or are severely suppressed.

Reply: I agree that labor unions are not encouraged and may be suppressed. But this is not a function of Fascism. Economies that run on free-market principles are not Fascist. They are Capitalist. There is a difference. While unions may be looked down on in Capitalist systems, they still exist. What is more important is that unionization is not the only form of representation of workers. I have worked for three American multinationals. Unions don't exist in these organizations. They don't need to. Why? Because employee engagement can still take place without the need for formalized unions. The old confrontational nature between unions and the '*bourgeois*' management disappears when all employees have a stake in the organization. During the 1997

UK General Election, I attended a meeting organized by the local Labour Party. The Socialist audience and a Labour MP criticized the Conservative government's privatization programs. One woman stood up and said that under Socialism, workers own the means of production; that they have s stake. I was going to correct her. In hindsight, I should have, despite being the only Conservative in the room. The claim that workers own and run companies under Socialist principles is the most incredible illusion that Socialism has shown. Workers do not have a stake in the companies they work for. The companies would be nationalized, which means the GOVERNMENT, or the STATE owns the firms, NOT workers. The Socialist vision of ownership of companies by workers can be elegantly realized through the Capitalist principles of share ownership. Anyone can be a shareholder and can collectively influence decision-making at the board level. State-owned firms would not afford these luxuries to their workers. How has Trump attacked workers and employees?

11. Disdain for Intellectuals and the Arts — Fascist nations tend to promote and tolerate open hostility to higher education, and academia. It is not uncommon for professors and other academics to be censored or even arrested. Free expression in the arts and letters is openly attacked.

Reply: When did Trump express disdain for the Arts and higher education? By the way, the Trump administration has arrested professors and academics? Trump did extend funding for HCBUs (Historically Black Colleges and Universities) and support the Schools Choice program to help underprivileged children attend charter schools or private schools. Ethnic minorities that lag behind would benefit from this. This is similar to the UK Conservative Government's 'Assisted Places Scheme' during the 1990s, where bright children from poor families could attend private schools through a voucher scheme. It gave a choice to parents to send their children to private schools of their choice. One of my friends told me that he was a beneficiary of the Assisted Places Scheme, which helped him to attend a private boarding school. He then went on to attend a good university and subsequently worked for top consulting firms. I am proud of his achievement. Unfortunately, the scheme was abolished by the Labour Government in the late 1990s. Here is a stark contrast between Conservatives and Socialists. Conservatives will offer a helping hand so that people can progress and succeed on their own, whereas Socialism seeks to keep poor people equally poor and dependent on the state. Back to Trump. How does he fit into criteria no. 11?

12. Obsession with Crime and Punishment — Under fascist regimes, the police are given almost limitless power to enforce laws. The people are often willing to overlook police abuses and even forego civil liberties in the name of patriotism. There is often a national police force with virtually unlimited power in fascist nations.

Reply: This applies to America, how? The police in the US have always had powers regardless of who has been President. Don't police in communist or Socialist countries have massive powers? China comes to mind. Why isolate Fascists? And why isolate Trump, especially when he said that there needs to be police reform after the tragic murder of George Floyd? In America, people are not often willing to overlook police abuses. Many such police officers do get charged.

13. Rampant Cronyism and Corruption — Fascist regimes almost always are governed by groups of friends and associates who appoint each other to government positions and use governmental power and authority to protect their

friends from accountability. It is not uncommon in fascist regimes for national resources and even treasures to be appropriated or even outright stolen by government leaders.

Reply: How has Trump stolen national resources and treasures? How does the initial part of the criteria apply to Trump when some of his appointed associates later criticized him (Michael Cohen, Anthony Scaramucci, Michael Wolff, etc.)?

14. Fraudulent Elections — Sometimes, elections in fascist nations are a complete sham. Other times elections are manipulated by smear campaigns against or even assassination of opposition candidates, use of legislation to control voting numbers or political district boundaries, and manipulation of the media. Fascist nations also typically use their judiciaries to manipulate or control elections.

Reply: Smear campaigns happen on both sides. Charging Trump with white supremacy or Fascism is a massive smear, given that he does not seem to have fulfilled the 14 criteria laid out. Neither Trump nor any other President had control over political district boundaries. Do you believe Trump is manipulating the media? If so, how? The way I see it from the UK, it is the other way round. The mainstream media, like CNN, lambasts Trump, at every opportunity. How does Trump manipulate CNN? Presidents do not control elections in the US. How is Trump using the judiciary to manipulate the upcoming elections?

Conclusion

Back to you, Larry. You did cite the '*14 criteria for Fascism*' website a few times when you responded to other commentators who questioned the claim of Trump's Fascism. You diligently erased the word 'nutter' in my case when you pasted the same paragraphs from similar responses to Trump supporters. I thank you for this. It means we can have a good basis to engage in fruitful debate and dialogue. Looking at the 14 criteria for Fascism that Lawrence Britt laid out, you stated, '***Trump does come across as a classic Fascist.***' I have responded to every criterion. I would like to know your thoughts on my initial response, where I stated the racism that Joe Biden demonstrated. And why an apparent Fascist like Trump would implement policies to empower black America. I believe there is a 15th criterion for Fascism, and that is Anti-Semitism or hatred of Jews (as well as non-Whites). We can agree on this. Again, Trump beats the odds here. He was able to achieve two peace deals between Israel and its Arab neighbors, the UAE, and Bahrain. If he was a Fascist, he would have armed the Arab nations to the hilt and drive out the Jews to the sea. Remarkable, isn't it?

I liked your invocation of '***Hitchen's Razor***' in a comment you made elsewhere. The late Christopher Hitchens stated, '*what can be asserted without evidence can be dismissed without evidence.*' Allow me to metamorphosize 'Hitchen's Razor' to '***Hasan's Razor.***' This is where I state, '*what you have asserted without evidence, I have dismissed WITH evidence.*' Over to you now, Larry. I look forward to further engagements.

Note: After three attempts to get a response from Larry, the dialogue ended.

Donald Trump – The Enigma

If I were American, I would have voted for Hillary Clinton in 2016. I have always described myself as an anti-Trump Conservative, and I did agree with Marco Rubio when he stated in 2016 that Trump was not a true Conservative. What started as my absolute hatred for Trump over the last few years since 2016, has now changed to a position of neutrality. This neutrality is comprised of positives and negatives. The positives being the policies he has been able to implement at warp speed, which has benefited many people. The negatives being the bizarre statements Trump has made, coupled with his narcissism. The fact that some of his ex-aides, such as Michael Cohen, Anthony Scaramucci, and Michael Wolff, who have heavily criticized Trump's personality, cannot be ignored. Neither can we ignore Trump's strong criticisms made by Conservative doyens such as Colin Powell, Mitt Romney, George W. Bush, and the late John McCain. That is why President Trump remains an enigma.

E) *Are Pro-Trump Muslims 'Stupid Bastards?' Nuanced Insights into the US Elections 2020*

[This section is a follow on from my discussion on LBC Radio (UK) with the presenter, Maajid Nawaz, about the outcome of the US elections. Please listen to the 5-min discussion before reading further:
https://youtu.be/XiyTAJR3QEg]

What a way to start an article, with a very odd title. A well-known Muslim activist in America, Rabia Chaudry, who is an advocate of great stature, posted a very disheartened message on her Facebook page when everyone thought President Trump was on a winning streak. This is partly a response to her, as well as my insights into the Presidential elections following my discussion with LBC Radio's Maajid Nawaz.

Introducing the Greedy, Stupid Muslim Bastards

Rabia is well known for her documentary series about her client, Adnan Syed, who was jailed for the alleged murder of Hei Min Lee in 1999. Since then she has been trying to prove his innocence. Her documentary, 'Serial' was very popular and work has been done to get a re-trial for Adnan. I first came across her in 2017 during a scandal that hit the Muslim world when a well-known scholar and preacher, Nouman Ali Khan (NAK), had a photo of his beefy topless body leaked to the social media. The issue of alleged sexual harassment of a few women students came to the fore. I had written a 30-page open letter to Rabia and other Muslim activists and counsellors on how they mishandled the scandal; I also criticised NAK's followers for their woeful behaviour towards Rabia et al. because of their cult-like adulation of NAK.

The scandal had introduced me to the Muslim activists in the US, such as Rabia Chaudry, who was quite vocal in relation to alleged sexual harassment. A year later, during the Brett Kavanaugh-Christine Blasey Ford hearings, Rabia Chaudry, the MeToo movement and other groups fiercely condemned Brett Kavanaugh and believed that he had attempted to rape Ford. It doesn't matter which side of the debate you were on in relation to Kavanaugh-Ford; everyone will agree that sexual harassment of women is wrong. This is what the MeToo movement highlighted in 2018. Where is this leading and what has this got to do with the US elections? I hear you ask. I will pull it together, bear with me.

Imagine my puzzlement and incredulity when Rabia described Muslim Trump voters as *'greedy, stupid bastards.'* She even wished hell and damnation on those Muslims who voted for Trump, and that Trump's tax cuts would be devoid of 'barakah' (blessings). She wrote this at the time when people thought Trump was going to win the election. Why send fire and brimstones on these few Muslim Trump voters?

I came face to face with Muslim fanatics in 2005 when I stood for the British Parliament, as a Conservative candidate. A fanatical group, the Al-Muhajiroun, had a mugshot of me and other Muslim Parliamentary candidates on their website. They ex-communicated us because they believed that Muslims' participation in Western politics was *'haram'* (forbidden). I challenged them to a public debate and even offered for Sky News channel to cover this debate. But they backed down one week before the debate was due to take place. They had no legs to stand on, and there was absolutely no way I was going to allow them to get away in trying to link Islam/Quran with terrorism. Imagine my surprise when I came across Rabia's Facebook outburst. I will certainly not allow her to get away with an Islamophobic/racist comment like that. However, she is not in the same category as those Muslim fanatics I just mentioned. She is your bog-standard Muslim American...the Muslim version of motherhood and apple pie. There would be no difference between the Joneses and the Chaudrys.
But a peculiar phenomenon that I am witnessing from liberals and the far left (Muslim or otherwise) is rage politics and rationalised racism.

Most Muslims voted Democrat, but a few voted for Trump because they preferred his tax policy, i.e. tax cuts. Rabia lambasted these Muslims and South Asians who voted for this reason. Consider the phrase, *'**Greedy, Stupid Muslim Bastards'**.* Anything wrong with this phrase? No? Ok, let's leave aside Muslim Trump voters and look at Black Trump voters. In that same phrase, replace the word '***Muslim'**' with the word '***Black'**'. Now read the new phrase. Can you see the inherent racism breaking through and shining with shear resplendence? Whilst we are here, why not replace the word *'Muslim'* with *'Jewish'*, as there were Jewish Trump voters. Read the new phrase again. You can see antisemitism bursting out as well. This outburst is from the mouth (typing fingers actually) of a formidable lawyer, human rights activist and broadcaster. Her words in that Facebook post are like DNA strands that form the building blocks of rationalised racism. The fact that the word, *'Muslim'* is used instead of *'Black'* or *'Jewish'* somehow rationalises her racism, in this case Islamophobia. Rabia is a Muslim, but that does not make it ok. If she can call out some Muslims using Islamophobic terms, then this justifies and emboldens actual Islamophobes who seek to call out Muslims for other reasons.

The South Asian ethnicity has not been free to roam, they too were targeted in this racist outburst if they voted for Trump. *'Greedy, Stupid, South Asian and Muslim Bastards'*. This is the summary of her Facebook outburst. Re-read this phrase and ask yourself if Donald Trump has ever uttered words like these on fellow Americans. It is true that Trump did target the Muslim Representative Ilhan Omar in some of his campaign rallies and charged her for not being patriotic, and her apparent preference of Yemen to the US (even though she is from Somalia). His attack on Ilhan Omar was unnecessary and he fell into the trap of giving the oxygen of publicity to her and the rest of the far left's 'Squad', that they crave for. Whatever combinations, permutations and iterations of Trumps words against Omar and the squad we can juggle around, they would not spell out the incendiary paraphrase *'greedy, stupid South Asian (or) Muslim bastards.'* But Trump is the one who has been called out for Islamophobia and even White supremacy despite condemning it a few times, yet Rabia's racist outburst seems to be acceptable and rationalised. If this is her view of pro-Trump South Asians and Muslims, then one can only imagine what she and the left think of Black Republicans and Jewish Republicans.

Rage, Racism and Chauvinism — The New Narrative of the Far Left

Over the last few months after the tragic murder of George Floyd, I began to notice a new narrative rising in the left/far left, the racism of groupthink and their rage to justify it. I dealt with this in detail in my book, *'United States of Anger'*. It is a narrative that states that your skin colour or religion should determine how you vote. If you are Black or Asian/Latino or Muslim, then you have to vote Democrat. I faced this odd racist narrative in the 1990s when I joined the UK Conservative Party. The Labour Party was seen as a party of the Asians and that I should have joined them. I chose to remain within the Conservative Party and never looked back.

When some Muslims or Blacks or Asians or even women decide to fly the nest of the left's groupthink and join Conservatives/Republicans, they are attacked. The latent racism within the far left do not remain latent anymore. And what has surprised me is the anti-woman chauvinism I witnessed among some feminists, which is very odd if not paradoxical. If women join Conservatives (Trump or no Trump), they are accused of propping up patriarchy and White supremacy. Judge Amy Coney Barrett is a case in point. She was an excellent pick by Donald Trump, and I watched her performance during the senate hearings when she was cross examined by Democrat senators. The tactics of the Democrats fell apart like dominoes when Barrett held her ground....even against Kamala Harris, whose precision questioning of Brett Kavanaugh in 2018 left him flustered. Barrett is the one who had balls of steel compared to Kavanaugh. The chauvinism is this. Feminists hate her for representing a narrative which their own grandmothers adhered to with pride; of having a large family, maintaining family values and maintaining religious tradition. The feminist author, Lauren Hough, describe Judge Barrett as a *'handmaid with a car clown vagina'*. This phrase means she birthed lots of children. And a laughable extreme version of the left's narrative about Barrett is that she adopted Black Haitian children in order to instill White supremacy values! True. The adoption of these Black children has obviously nothing to do with giving these kids from poor backgrounds a nice home in the US with a loving, Christian family. Barret gave birth to five children. Instead of giving birth, if she had five abortions, she would have been a superhero of the far left because she would have exercised reproductive freedom. Sad but true. Muslims, Asians, Latinos and Africans should bear in mind that Hough's attack on Barrett's multiple births is an attack on our communities too, where we tend to have higher birth rates compared to our White counterparts. The White supremacy terrorist, Brenton Tarrant, who killed 50 Muslims in New Zealand in 2019, expressed his frustration with high Muslim birth rates in his White supremacy trash, '**The Great Replacement Manifesto'** (which is thankfully no longer available online). Hough and Tarrant represent two extreme sides of the same coin, the far left and the far right. One has used abusive language to prove her point and the other has used a gun to prove his point.

Insight into the US Elections

This long preamble on the far left's racism and chauvinism leads me nicely to the main part of this article, which is my insights into the US election. It is very short and simple. **I congratulate President-elect Joe Biden and Kamal Harris. May God guide his presidency and bless America.** This is what President Trump should have said. He should have conceded like a man and give his full support to the President-elect by granting him access to the daily briefings, for starters. I agree with LBC Radio's Maajid Nawaz, when he told me that Trump had every right to pursue a legal course. In principle, he is correct. There is the legal route and there is the ethical/moral route. Yes, Trump has the right to initiate legal action BUT HE DOES NOT HAVE TO. He can take the ethical route and accept that the unity of America surpasses the position of the Presidency. The longer Trump leaves it, the more he will be remembered for his child-like bluster, narcissism, obnoxious behaviour (some psychiatrists told me that he has personality disorder issues) and living in denial instead of his legacies, of which there are many. Furthermore, Trump supporters who treat Trump like a Messianic cult leader, need to come back to reality and accept that the most powerful country in the world will be led by Biden and Harris (eventually Harris, as Biden's cognitive decline slides further down). I made this point in a Conservative social group. I didn't get much pushback. Trump supporters also need to have a moment of self-reflection when they claim to be true American patriots. They will recall in 2016 when Trump urged Russians to hack into Hillary Clinton's computer and find her deleted emails. When an American presidential candidate asks a foreign adversary to hack into the computer of a fellow American who was a former First Lady, THIS IS TREASON. Trump supporters should be true patriots and call out Trump for his incitement to foreign interference.

Both Democrats and Republicans were wrong when they thought their own parties would win by a landslide. Pollsters clearly underestimated Trump in Florida and Ohio...the states which CNN anchors said would be needed to clinch the presidency. It was a bad night for Trump but good for Republicans as they gained more senate seats. Both parties had good news and bad news. I hope Biden is true to his words and starts the process of uniting Americans. In my book, *'United States of Anger'*, I stated that there were a few

Democrat policies that I agreed with, such as, universal healthcare, restricting handguns and taking Covid-19 more seriously. But Trump should be remembered for the positive policies he has implemented. Pro-Trump Muslims may have voted for Trump for policies other than tax cuts. Some of these policies are listed below, and President-elect Biden should build on these when he takes office. And I will link these to Rabia's terminology of '**Muslim, South Asian greedy bastards...(deserving of) hellfire.**' You can then ascertain who the real bastards are. I won't ascertain anything as I don't name-call, I engage in positive discourse with whom I disagree with.

Some Achievements of President Trump

1. Increasing employment among Blacks and Latinos before the Covid pandemic hit.

2. Increasing long term funding for HBCUs (Historically Black Colleges and Universities).

3. First Step Act to reduce incarcerations of Black prisoners. President Clinton did admit that the 1994 Crime Bill (which caused the increased incarcerations) was a mistake.

4. Helping business owners (including Black business owners) to get on their feet after violent protesters burnt them down.

5. Largest increase of BAME (Black, Asian Minority Ethnic) people within the Republican Party since the 1960s. In my book, I stated that the Republican Party is the home of BAME communities. The creation of the Republican was solely based on the abolition of slavery. It has a proud foundation to fall back on. Democrats do not have this foundation as they

have been traditionally been the party of slavery, lynching, KKK and segregation. Trump should have highlighted the GOP's strong foundation of diversity and inclusion during his campaigns.

6. Increase in women's employment.

7. *Covid Pandemic*. It is still unclear how Trump handled the pandemic in its totality, so I am not sure whether this is an achievement. There are two issues that have run in parallel with each other, a success and a failure. The first is his failure to communicate the seriousness of the pandemic and his flirtation with some of the conspiracy theory sceptics about Covid-19, in that the risk-mitigation restrictions was an attack on freedom. Wrong. And I am with the Democrats on this one. Trump could have handled communications better and treat Americans as adults by explaining the risks of the virus and the need for wearing masks and social distancing. The second issue is the imminent success of *'Operation Warp Speed.'* This is where Trump's administration spent billions of dollars to help many pharmaceutical companies develop vaccines in a short period of time with purchase agreements and logistics in place. When Trump announced a few months ago that a vaccine would be available by the end of this year, I was sceptical. Having worked in the pharmaceutical industry for over 20 years I knew it takes years to bring a new drug to market from the time the phase 3 trials are completed. I knew Operation Warp Speed tasked many pharmaceutical companies to reduce this time gap, but when Trump said a few months ago about a possible vaccine to market by November, I did not believe him because of his tendencies to exaggerate along with the timing of coinciding with the election. I thought he was trying to make political capital out of this. When Pfizer recently announced the successful results of its phase 3 trial of a candidate vaccine where it is 90% effective, I was very pleased because it meant

that millions of patients' lives would be saved. I then remembered Trump's promise he made a few months ago; he was right and I was wrong. The purchase agreement which is part of Operation Warp Speed helped Pfizer to make a huge investment in the development of its vaccine with the guarantee that the US Government would purchase 100 million doses amounting to nearly $2 bn. We should give credit where it is due. And when other pharmaceutical companies announce their successes, many more lives will be saved. And the time gap has been reduced by a few years. This would be one of the major legacies of Trump as he exits the presidency, to know that he would be partly responsible for the saving of millions of lives over the next few years which would overshadow the hundreds of thousands of excess deaths that have taken place in the US during 2020 because of Trump's mismanagement of advice around protection during the pandemic.

That being said, it will be difficult for President-elect Biden to find faults with Operation Warp Speed. Apparently, Biden's adviser, Dr. Celine Gounder, said that this operation needs to be overhauled. I was dubious and curious about this claim. But when I read an article on this, it turns out that the 'overhaul' is not really an overhaul. None of the projects agreed with pharmaceutical companies will be cancelled, but that there would be more spending on testing and tracing. Great. Biden can build on Trump's success on Operation Warp Speed.

—— —— —— —— —— —— —— —— —— —— —— —— ——

(*Sense check*: if voters voted for Trump because of the above seven policies, *they are bastards because…?*)

8. *Israel peace deals*: Peace deals between Israel and the UAE, Bahrain, and Saudi Arabia will join soon. Peace is the only way forward to ensure that the lives of Palestinians improve and that tit-for-tat revenge by HAMAS and Israeli military, respectively, are prevented. Too many innocent lives have been lost because of the failure of politicians on both sides. The terrorist group, HAMAS, has let down the Palestinians since it was elected in 2006. It therefore falls upon the other Arab/Muslim nations to step in and work out peace deals with Israel so that peace can finally break out. Israel would also be accountable to these Muslim countries in how they treat Palestinians, e.g. the recent bulldozing some of the Palestinian houses by Israeli authorities would not happen. Before this, the Israeli Government was only accountable to the US. There is a religious angle here, and I mentioned this on radio a few weeks ago. If Saudi Arabia makes peace with Israel, to me it means that the land of The Prophet has reached out to the land of the prophets in Abrahamic brotherhood. What would prophet Abraham say if his descendants started to live in peace instead of fighting? And if some Muslims supported Trump because of the historic and unprecedented peace deals in the Middle East, *they are bastards because…..?*

It is interesting when Nancy Pelosi was asked about these peace deals, she described them as 'distractions.' I am certain if President Hillary Clinton had achieved these peace deals, Pelosi would have nominated her for the Nobel Peace prize.

9. *US military Intervention*: This issue is very peculiar, mind boggling and unusual from my perspective as a Muslim. The biggest gripe that the Muslim world had with America, was its military interventions around the world, especially the Middle East and Afghanistan. I recall the '*Stop the War Coalition*' protests in the UK, organised by Socialists and Muslim activists. There was resentment with the US governments for their involvement in wars and causing instabilities wherever they intervened. Trump had battled Pentagon generals on this very issue of military intervention. He did not like interventions and actually started to pull out

troops from Afghanistan and Iraq, neither did he initiate a new war. As late as 12th November 2020, there was an announcement of a purge of the pentagon, and that the retired colonel, Douglas McGregor, has been appointed to lead the accelerated withdrawal of troops. This is unprecedented when compared to his predecessors. For some reason this has not featured on the radar of the Muslim media. Muslim activists and even Socialist activists around the world seem to have been silent on this big, joyful elephant in the room. So, if some Muslims supported Trump because of less military intervention in Muslim countries, *they are bastards because…?*

In 2006 when I delivered a speech at our UK Conservative Party Conference, I openly criticised Madeline Albright, who was President Clinton's Secretary of State, for stating that the killing of 500,000 Iraqi children was justified (because of ensuing democracy). What label would Rabia Chaudry use to classify her? I could have misused the podium to call Albright a bastard, but in true civil fashion I called her by her title. How would Rabia Chaudry view Trump's reduced military presence around the world?

10. **Uyghur Muslims and the Sanctioning of China**: A big Muslim and human rights issue has been the detention of one million Uyghur Muslims in China in internment camps. Both Democrats and Republicans came together and voted for the Uyghur Human Rights Policy Act in June. Donald Trump signed this into law and issued economic sanctions against China. Understandably, this wasn't publicised because the protests post George Floyd's murder had taken hold around the world. But Muslim campaigners and activists, including Rabia Chaudry, had highlighted the plight of Uyghur Muslims. Here is the problem. At one point, Kamala Harris did not agree with the economic sanctions against China because it would increase consumer prices and affect

businesses in California. This objection runs in parallel, quite elegantly, to the 'greedy tax cut' objection. They are equivalent analogies. Muslims (and others) who voted for Trump's tax cuts are called greedy bastards because they were thinking of economic benefits. So, what would Kamala Harris be called when she used the same principle of economic benefit to object to economic sanctions against China?

Both the Democrat senators and Republican senators and Donald Trump should be recognised for this major milestone in the American defence of human rights. And if some Muslims voted for Trump because of his support of Uyghur Muslims in China, *they are bastards because…?*

11. **Life of the Unborn**. As a human race, we pride ourselves in living in the 21st Century, because of the advances we made through technology, social progress, economic progress and improvement of human rights. We call it the *'modern world.'* But in a marvelous and cognitive dissonant parallel, many pride themselves in the support of *'reproductive rights'* through the killing of unborn babies. This is the big red flag of human rights abuse that has ever been perpetrated against innocent human beings under the guise of women's rights. Most people on the left are pro-choice for abortion and most on the right are pro-choice for life. However, there are pro-life Democrats, but few in number. So, a big shout-out to *'Democrats For Life'*. One of their Zoom discussion videos, *'Black Lives Matter — A Whole Life Perspective'* is brilliant.
(link: https://www.facebook.com/watch/live/?v=233968437 3006873&ref=watch_permalink).

Unfortunately, that video had only 18 likes at the time of writing this article, a sad reflection of the pro-choice for abortion psyche of the Democrat platform. **This issue is not**

a case of right vs left, it is a case of right VS wrong. Traditionally, Republican presidents have implemented pro-life policies and Democrat presidents less so. I recall that President Clinton once said that abortion should be *'safe, legal and rare'*. I agree with the first part and the last part. President George W. Bush did well to ban partial birth abortions and to also sign the *'**Born Alive Infant Protections Act'**￼* in 2002. He fulfilled his campaign promise during one of the presidential debates with Al Gore, that he wanted to create a culture of life.

However, I understand that President Trump went further than previous Republican presidents to protect the unborn and prevent their killing through reduced federal funding of abortion, and reduction of funding abortions abroad. This particular initiative abroad led Trump's critics to nickname it the *'global gag order.'* I welcomed the restrictions on abortion in Alabama, Ohio, Louisiana and abroad (although education on AIDS, HIV, contraception should still continue in poor countries). At the same time unfortunately, abortion was extended in Virginia under Gov. Ralph Northam and in New York under Gov. Andrew Cuomo. Interestingly, Cuomo condemned the death penalty for murderers as morally indefensible...work that one out. Most pro-choice for abortion supporters would have looked at Trump's defence of the unborn with absolute horror and disgust (I have read enough pro-choice literature and listened to many pro-choice advocates to understand how most of them would think). Pro-life campaigners would have welcomed restrictions in killing babies. President-elect Biden will reverse the progress that Trump had made in saving lives. For that, we can only apologise to thousands, if not millions of future innocent lives that will be erased as they leave this earth with silent screams.

It will take a long time for the ***Roe vs Wade 1973*** to be rescinded (same for the 1967 Abortion Act in the UK). One can only hope that Judge Amy Coney Barrett (and other judges) will do the right thing and protect unborn lives, assuming President Biden keeps her in the Supreme Court. **Before laws can be changed, minds need to be changed**. Many campaigners advocate for the protection of wildlife, protection of trees, banning of animal cruelty, calling world dictators to account for their human rights abuses; yet the tsunami waves of cognitive dissonance sweep through the minds of these very same campaigners when the topic of abortion arises. There is a massive disconnect somewhere in the synapses and neural pathways. This magnificent contradiction always has puzzled me until I learnt about historical campaigns for women's rights in America. In the 19th Century, one feminist campaigner, Elizabeth Cady Stanton, stated:

"We educated, virtuous white women are more worthy of the vote … What will we and our daughters suffer if these degraded black men are allowed to have the rights that would make them even worse than our Saxon fathers?"

This example demonstrates that people can advocate for one form of human right and another form of human wrong at the same time in the cognitive dissonant mind space. In the case of early White American feminists, they did not consider black women, let alone black men, to be deserving of human rights. Blacks were not even second class citizens because they occupied an untouchable space below any class. They were dehumanised. In a striking parallel with abortion, unborn babies/foetuses/embryos/bunch of cells/parasites are dehumanised. That is why it is easy for pro-abortion advocates to become immune to, and to live in denial of mass infanticide.

Dialogue and debate between pro-choice and pro-life groups are the only ways forward. I look back to the time I stood for Parliament in 2005 and regret not focusing on this issue more robustly. But I did engage with feminists on abortion and we have always been polite and civil to each other. I would look to similar positive engagements soon.

Conservatives need to be less judgemental of the left and feminists. And they need to be more patient and engage in positive discourses with them. We can draw inspiration from the debates between the Republican's Abraham Lincoln and the Democrat's Stephen Douglas in the 1850s. Lincoln advocated for abolition of slavery. Douglas was very articulate and erudite, and advocated for 'choice' (sound familiar?), that different states had a right to choose whether to end slavery or not. We can learn how Lincoln convinced people to humanise Black communities and get rid of slavery once and for all. He lost his life as a result when a Democrat/Confederate murdered him. It took about 100 years for the Democrats to shed its sordid attachment to slavery, racism and segregation. But the same mentality of de-humanising a group of humans (unborn babies) is a vestigial by-product of a by-gone era of human rights abuses. It may take another hundred years for the Democrats to shed their support of mass killing of unborn babies and finally look back to this era (as they look back now to the era of slavery) and ask themselves, *'how in God's name did we allow this to happen?'* The defeat of Trump and the election of Biden is a regressive setback to the culture of life. We Conservatives need to remove toxicity of this topic by engaging in positive discourse with whom we disagree with, because millions of future lives are depending on us. **HELP IS COMING**.

Back to Rabia Chaudry and the *'Muslim bastards'* issue. Muslims generally have been woefully silent on the injustices of killing unborn babies, and I call out my community for this. I believe that Rabia is pro-life. So, if some Muslims voted for Trump because of his defence of innocent lives, *they are bastards because…?* Surely there is 'barakah' (blessings) in the saving of lives?

Are there any Democrat Muslim Bastards?

I don't name-call. As I have been critical of Trump in some aspects and supportive of him on other aspects, we can apply the same standard with Biden's Democrats. Earlier, I stated a few Democrat policies I agree with. There are of course many things I disagree with. I won't list them all here but will focus on three things.

1. Racism. I alluded to racist elements within the far left earlier in the article and in my book. I won't rehash them here. But you will recall during the Democrat primaries that Kamala Harris had accused Biden of racism (in the issue of busing) when he supported two pro-segregation senators. Harris laid in to him big time, so much so that the other Democrat contender, Tulsi Gibbard (my favourite Democrat) called out Harris for her attack. This means Harris really believed in what she said when she accused Biden of racism even though she did try to dismiss this during Stephen Corbett's show after she was selected as Biden's running mate. Biden also made a racist statement on Charlamagne Da god's podcast when he said that if Black voters could not decide between Trump and Biden, that they were not Black. The Black rapper, 50 Cent, was also patronised by the White comedian, Chelsea Handler, who reminded him that he was Black and therefore should not support Trump. Under the green field of the Democrats' diversity, there are landmines of racism buried underneath.

So, when many Muslims and non-Muslims voted for Joe Biden knowing about the racist statements he made, what term would our illustrious advocate, Rabia Chaudry, use to describe these voters thereby withdrawing 'barakah' (blessings) and sending them to Hellfire?

2. **Sexual Harassment**. I used the term 'cognitive dissonance' to highlight the contradiction between the Democrats' formidable positions on civil rights issues, and their support of killing of unborn babies if mothers and fathers so wish. Another marvelous cognitive dissonance I have seen emerge recently within the Democrat mindset is in relation to sexual harassment of women. Their tacit support of Christine Blasey Ford and condemnation of Brett Kavanaugh as a guilty party to attempted rape of Ford, was quite pronounced. And Kamala Harris and other would-be Democrat presidential nominees stated they believed Ford. The MeToo movement campaigned hard in 2018 to highlight the issue of such harassment against women. I supported this movement.

After the Ford-Kavanaugh hearings were over, Democrats forgot about Christine Ford and she still remains in hiding. Come 2020, the Democrats did a 180-degree U-Turn by refusing to support Tara Reade in her allegations of digital rape by Biden in 1993. What is going on here? Millions of Democrats remained silent on this issue apart from a few Socialists who are pro-Bernie Sanders. In my book I capture the short dialogue that I had with a Socialist acquaintance in the US. She, too, was disappointed with the complete silence of Biden supporters. Out of the 78 million people (mostly Democrats) who voted for Biden, only ONE Democrat Biden supporter called herself out for her hypocrisy. Meet Julianna Jana Young. She wrote an article on Medium.com entitled, *'Voting for Biden Means Owning My Hypocrisy.'* She has been honest about her vote for Biden knowing full well about the allegations against him by Tara Reade. I quote a part of her statement:

"But now, when our candidate is in the hot seat, we're slinking into the shadows and looking away. It wasn't too long ago that we were crucifying Brett Kavanaugh. We rallied behind Dr. Christine Blasey Ford and, despite inconsistencies, were disgusted with those who dared say she was making it up. Now, when it's time to rally behind Tara Reade, we're either not showing up, or performing some double-speak dance of, 'We believe women, except when it's Joe Biden.'"

Julianna is 1 in 78 million. I commend her honesty. For the rest of the 74,999,999 million voters who voted for Biden in silence, knowing about these serious allegations....what type of exotic nomenclature would our esteemed advocate, Rabia Chaudry, use to describe these pro-Biden Muslim voters? I won't call them bastards. They are just Democrat voters who sacrificed one of their bedrock principles in order to gain power.

3. **Life Again**. The issue of abortion was dealt with extensively earlier. There were some Muslims and non-Muslims who voted for Trump in order to defend the rights of the unborn. Biden will undo these rights and reverse Trump's policies. Civil rights will regress, not progress. Many Muslims would have voted for Biden knowing full well that thousands and possibly millions of unborn babies would be killed because it would be easier to do so under the Biden-Harris administration. What wonderful expletives would our human rights advocate (who I believe is pro-life), Rabia Chaudry, use to describe these Muslims? What would the withdrawal of 'barakah' (blessings) and the threat of Hellfire look like for these voters because of their support of the killing of innocent lives?

What Type of Muslim Bastard Am I?

You tell me. I am a Conservative and a Republican supporter from across the pond. Am I pro-Trump? Difficult to say. Over the last few years, I had been on radio many times to state categorically that if I was American, I would have voted for Hillary Clinton in 2016. During this period, I must have lambasted Donald Trump at least six or seven times claiming that he was not a Conservative or that he was a racist and a White supremacist. Only in the last two months have I been introduced to Trump's actual policies that have benefitted many people. In my book, '*United States of Anger*', the reader will see this transition from an anti-Trump position to a neutral position. This neutrality is composed of plusses and minuses of Trump. I would liken Trump to a mad scientist. He may have strokes of genius on good days cocooned inside a shell of narcissism, notoriety and personality disorder. That is why the last sub-chapter in my book is entitled, '*Donald Trump, the Enigma*.' I have not been able to state in that book or in this article who I would have voted for in 2020 if I was an American citizen. It is very difficult, knowing the pros and cons of both candidates. The identity of my preferred candidate remains unclear to me, but is irrelevant now. The election is over. The litigations are unlikely to help Donald Trump. He should do the right thing and concede graciously to Joe Biden and help support his presidency for the sake of all Americans, and for the sake of the world.

Final word about Rabia Chaudry and name-calling. In my view, racist name-calling is not necessary when good arguments are ready to be deployed. I have deployed them here profusely and elsewhere. And I invite my fellow American-Pakistani sister to engage her legal mind and optimise her legal acumen to respond to a fellow British-

Bangladeshi brother across the pond; who has argued convincingly why Muslims and South Asians who voted for Trump are not greedy, stupid bastards.

My Damascene journey toward conversion to Trump may have started, albeit very late when he is preparing to hand over the presidency to Joe Biden. The road is still bumpy, but my mind is open to be swayed either way, all the more reason why dialogue and debate are necessary. This has been the intention of this book, and I hope and pray that Linda Sarsour or her fellow comrades will continue the dialogue. Let's see where this journey takes us, *inshallah* (God willing). In the meantime, I hope that other readers, who are on the left or independent, have made a seismic shift or even a quantum shift toward Conservatism. It will be difficult to disagree with a lot of the points I have made, but I am all ears. Let's continue the debate.

ABOUT THE AUTHOR

 Hasan Ali Imam was born in Bangladesh and had been living in the UK for 46 years. He has been engaged in debate and dialogue over the last 30 years, culminating in his candidacy for the British Parliament in 2005. He continues to be involved with the UK Conservative Party in his spare time, while working full-time for a multinational corporation. Hasan has also been involved with the UK Government's 'Prevent' counter-terrorism strategy as a 'Trainer' to public servants on preventing young people, who may be Muslims or on the far right, walking down the path towards radicalization. He also draws on his own experience of attempted recruitment by extremist groups in the 1990s, including a terrorist who was later involved in the murder of an American journalist, Daniel Pearl. Hasan regularly takes part in discussions on radio and TV in the UK and writes articles on various platforms. His main passion resides in politics and hopes to become a Member of Parliament one day.

Printed in Great Britain
by Amazon